Jukebox Jive

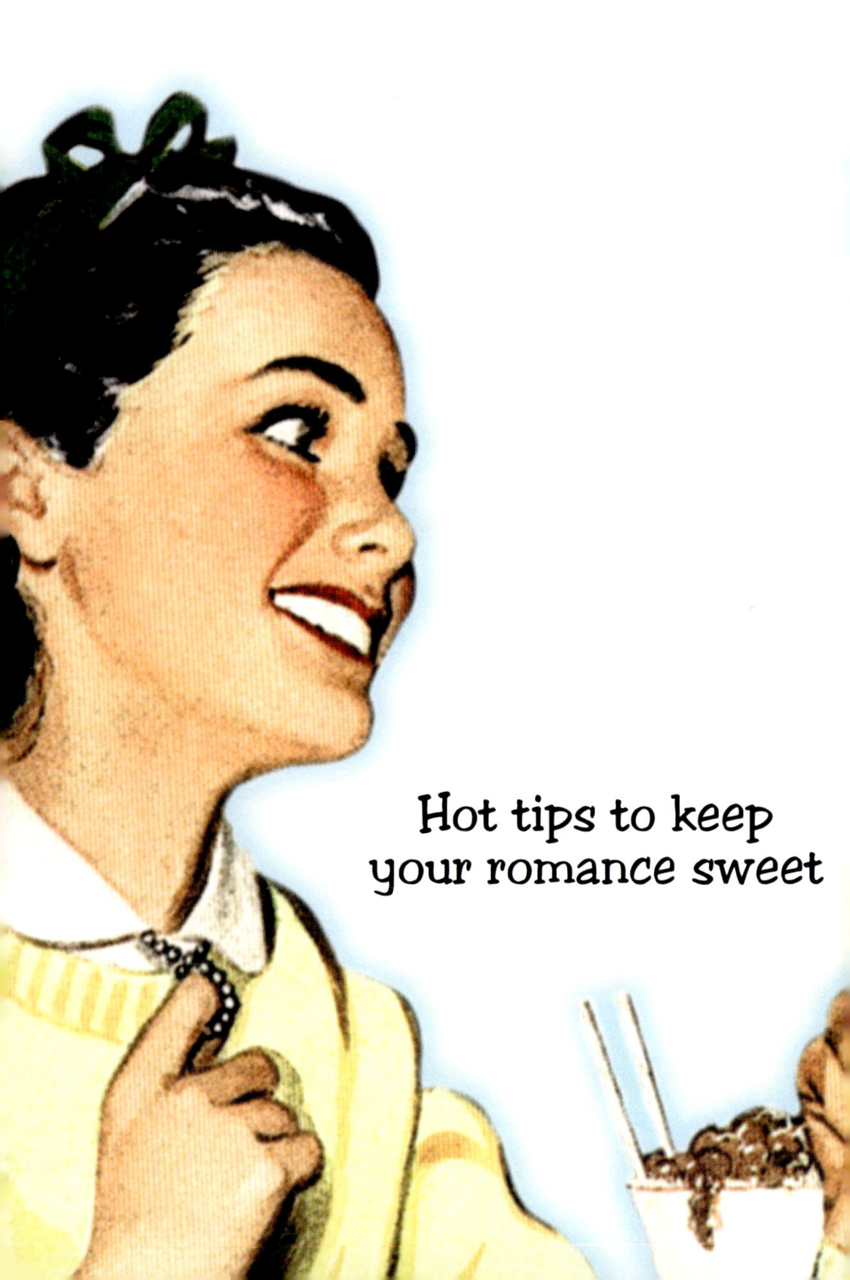
Hot tips to keep
your romance sweet

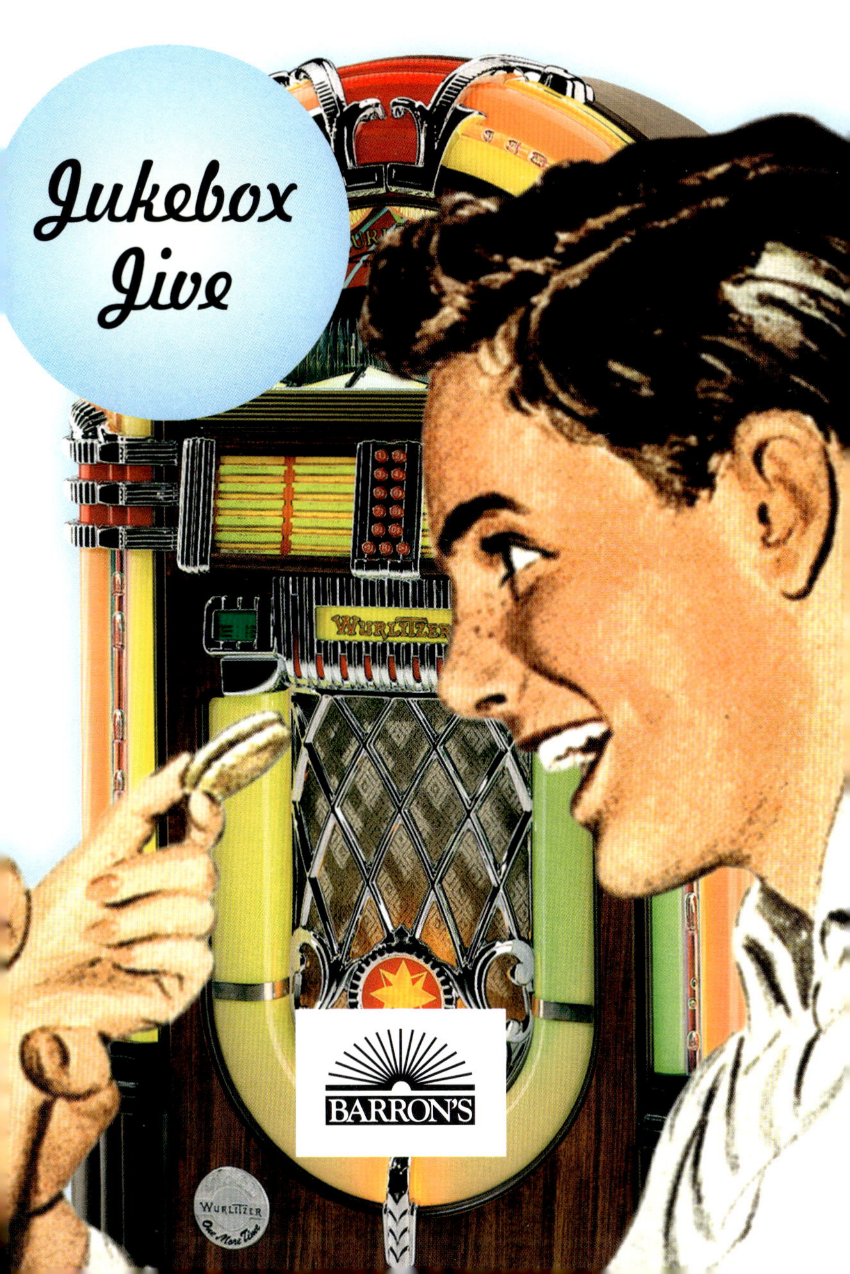
Jukebox
Jive
WURLITZER
BARRON'S
WURLITZER
One More Time

First edition for North America published in 2004
by Barron's Educational Series, Inc.

All inquiries should be addressed to:
Barron's Educational Series, Inc.
250 Wireless Boulevard
Hauppauge, NY 11788
http://www.barronseduc.com

International Standard Book No. 0-7641-2727-6
Library of Congress Catalog Card No. 2003109650

Text compilation: Yvonne Deutch
Series Editor: Yvonne Deutch
Design: Lindsey Johns

Printed in China
9 8 7 6 5 4 3 2 1

Welcome to jukebox jive

Slip a nickel into the magic jukebox of happiness, and enter the golden world of *Jukebox Jive*. Here, in this sweet and stylish retro celebration, you'll bop at the sock hop, jive and jitterbug until you drop, play it cool doing the stroll or the Madison, then clap your hands, and learn to do the twist again! Join those groovy guys and gals of the 1950s as they hit the scene in roaring hot rods, and drove down Main with radios

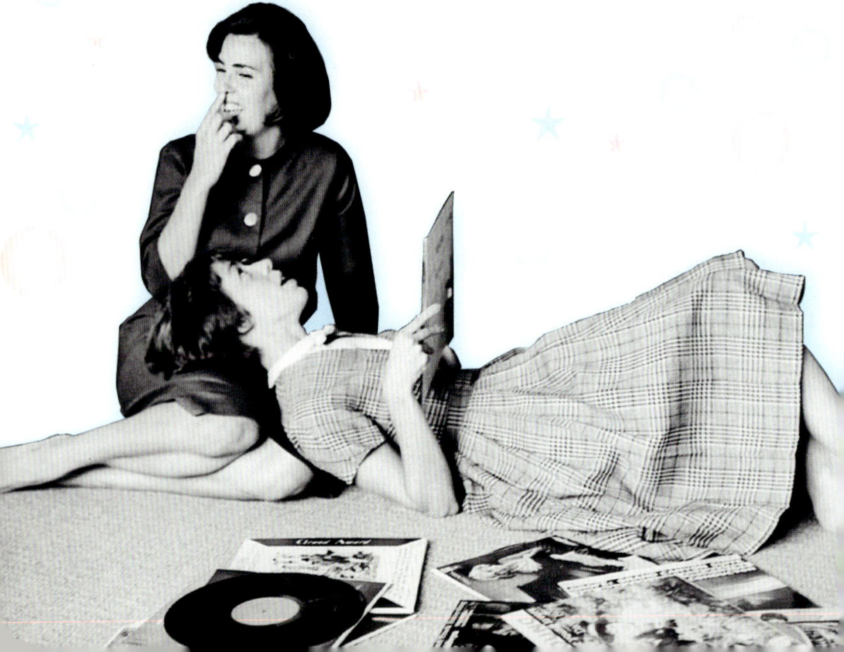

blaring out the latest hits from Elvis, Chuck Berry, Ricky Nelson, Buddy Holly, the Everly Brothers, Johnny Mathis, and Pat Boone. And if they were a tad rebellious and misunderstood, so what? They had heroes like James Dean and Elvis who spoke up for them.

What a time to be young! Teenagers were now official! They had money to spend, places to go, dates to make, fun to enjoy, and style to follow. Getting the right look was crucial—letterman sweaters, pegged jeans, white T-shirts, flattops and pompadours for boys; saddle oxfords, bobby socks, ponytails, and wide skirts for girls.

And the pulse of love and romance beat its passionate rhythm. Teenagers were now dating when very young—but what were the rules? What to say? How far to go? How late to stay out? Runaround Sue has the classic scoop on what to do. Her "yakkety yak" delivers the latest buzz. She has plenty of hot tips to keep romance sweet—from how to get a boy to notice you, to fixing your hair just right! So, what are you waiting for, let's rock!

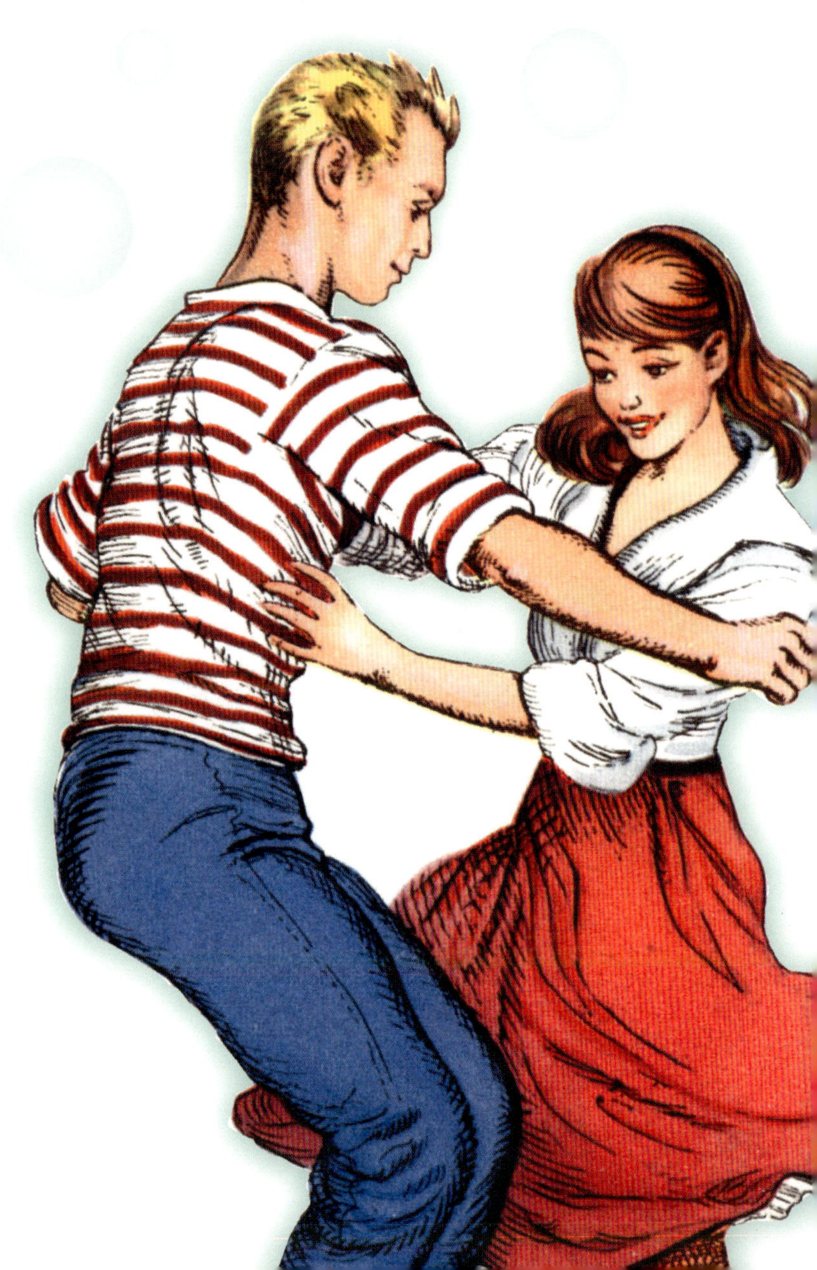

Chapter 1

AT THE HOP

Fingers clicking, feet jumping, hair flying, and eyes sparkling, 1950s teenagers were dance crazy! Whether it was a sock hop at the school gym, a spontaneous get together in the street, or even a formal high school prom, they rocked, jived, jitterbugged, and twisted the night away! Keen fans kept right up to date with the latest cool moves by watching the rave TV show, American Bandstand. New dances and hit songs kept on coming—and, as fast as they came, the kids were out there, grooving and dancing.

With rock and roll I have a ball,
Though father says I shouldn't,
He doesn't dig that jazz at all,
And if he did…I wouldn't!

Starlife Magazine, 1959

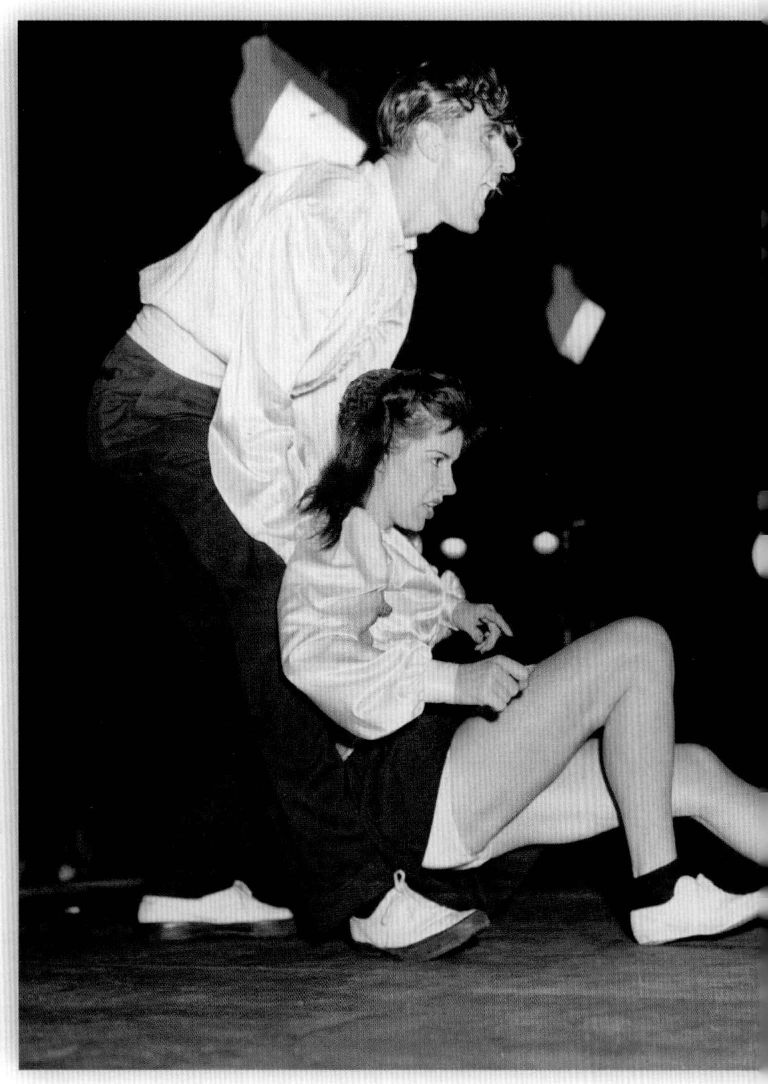

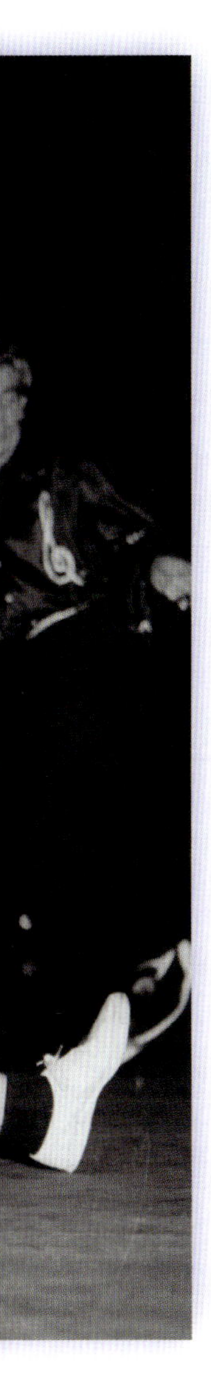

jitterbug

Bobby socks, saddle shoes, poodle skirts, oh so sweet.
Penny loafers and sock hops, the jitterbug...our beat.

Varsity sweaters with letters you'd earn,
and that '55 Chevy...the rubber she'd burn.

Cool leather jackets and pants that were pegged,
heavy greased ducktails. Our parents felt plagued!

A brightly lit jukebox. . .maybe "Heartbreak Hotel,"
the "King," Elvis Presley...Gee he was swell.

The Platters, the Chordettes; how they could sing,
and we'd hit the dance floor. Boy, could we swing!

Samantha S

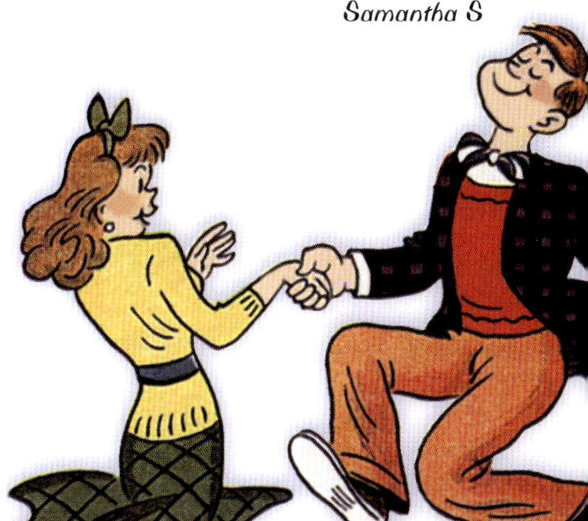

at the sock hop

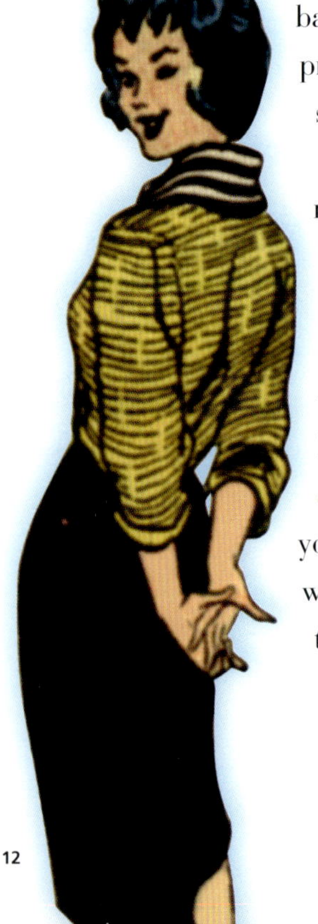

Sock hops weren't so bad, because they were informal, but the first few dances were terrifying. The guys would all line up on one side of the gym in our socks and the girls would line up on the other side in theirs. The term "wallflower" had real meaning. We pressed our backs against the wall, as if it could protect us. The girls looked us over, speculatively. We did our best not to look any of them in the eye. If you did meet their eyes, you were dead. You had to dance with the girl or look like a jerk. So the girls looked at us and we looked at the floor. Sometimes you did want to dance with a girl, but you knew that if you did, if you actually crossed the floor to ask her to dance, all your buddies would be on you when it was over. So you waited for someone else to dance first.

Larry Martin

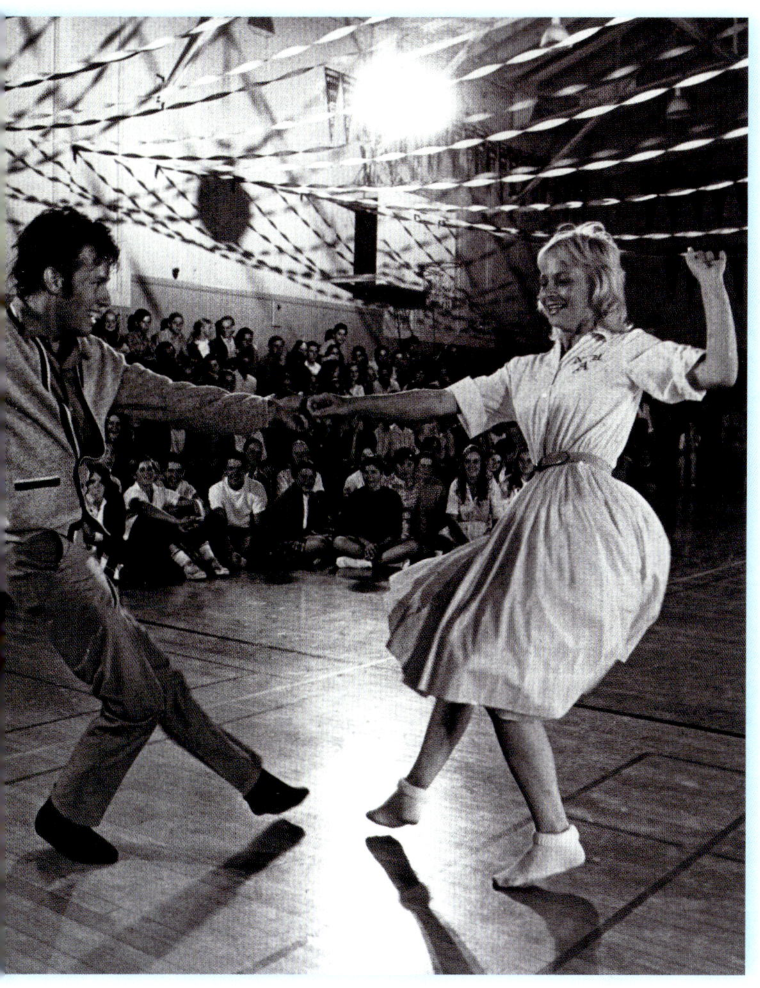

dancing in the street!

The best dances were in the street. They'd close off a street in the project and someone would set up a record player on a porch, and we'd dance. The streetlights would be on, but it was easy to dance out of the light. In the winter, we had dances after home basketball games, in the gym. If we won, everyone was in a good mood and we could really dance. If we lost, they'd play a lot of slow songs and we could dance close.

Mike Forrester

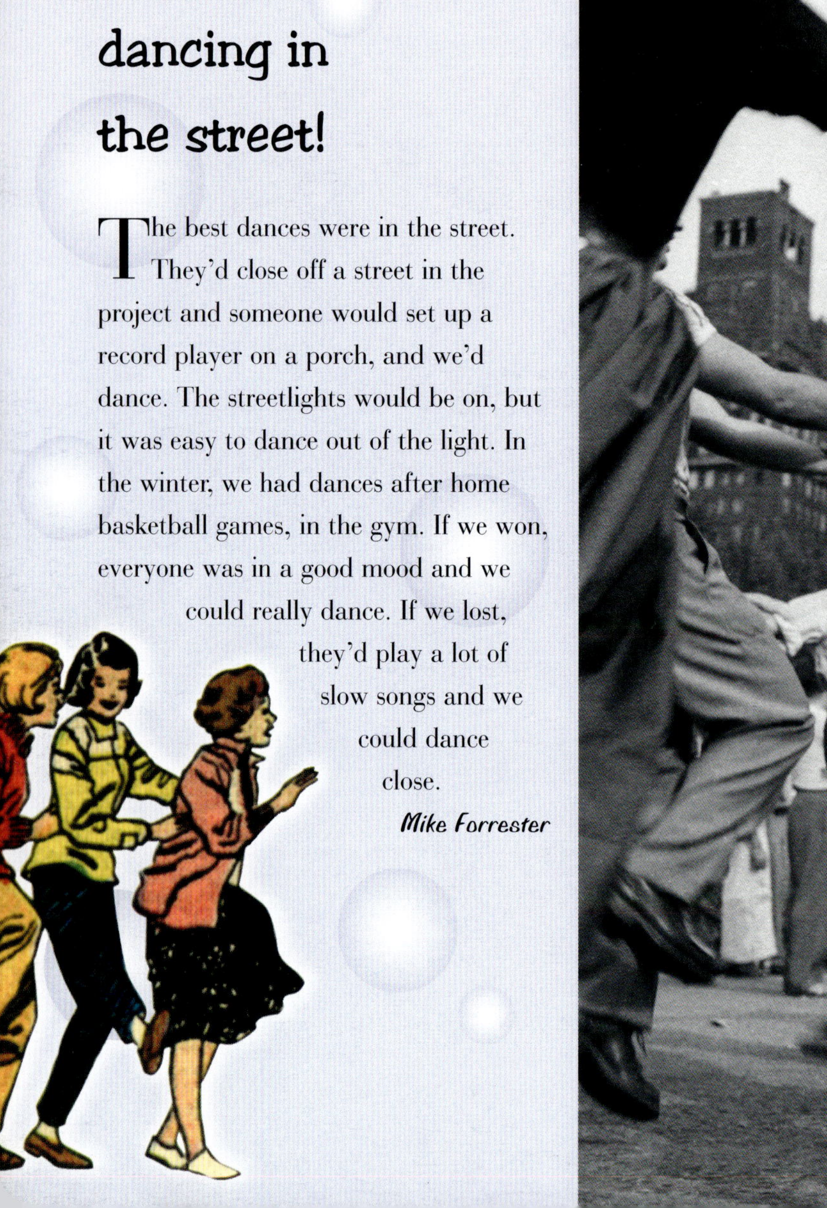

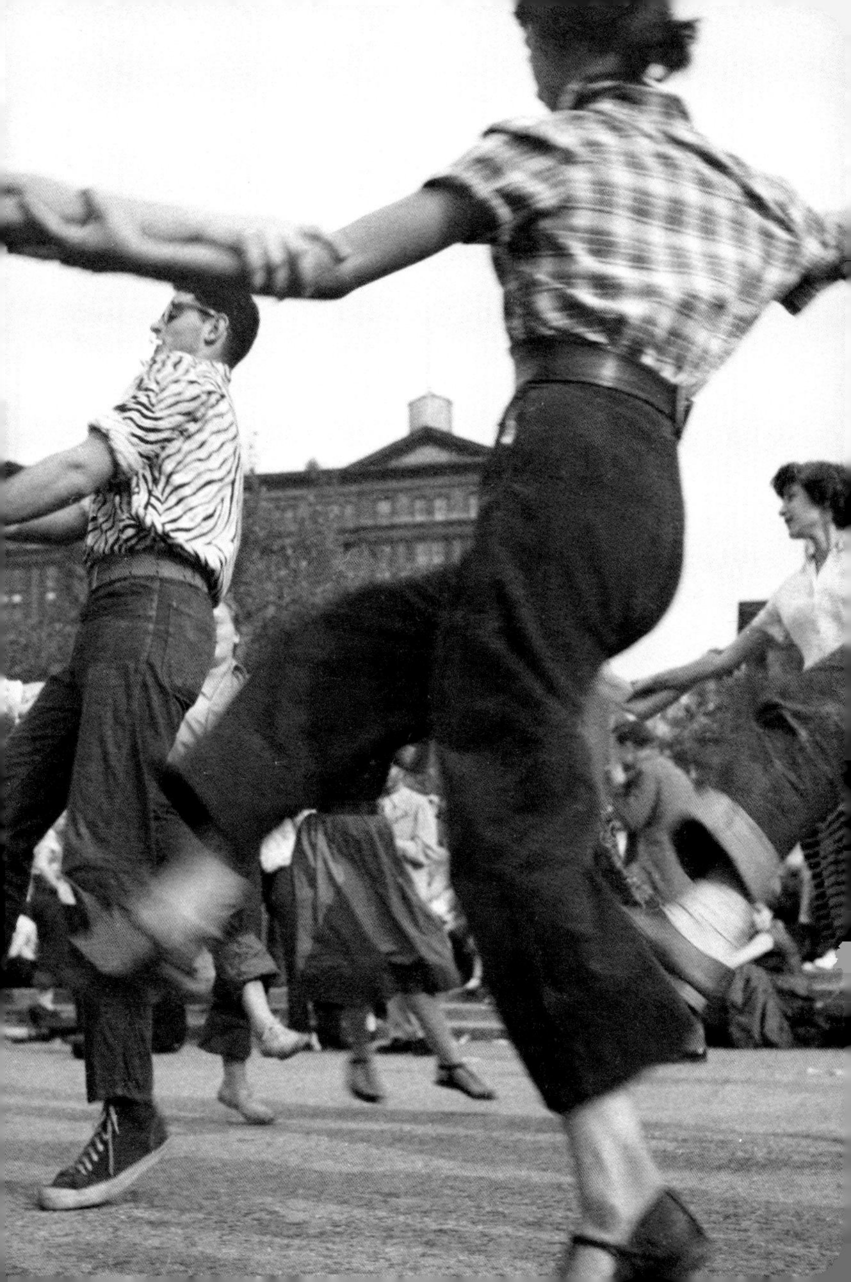

play it cool!

The boys my age were too shy to dance, so if you wanted to dance—and we all did—you had to catch the attention of an upper classman. They hung out in a different part of the gym, but fortunately, it was on the way to the ladies. So a friend of mine and I would comb our hair, put on the lipstick we were forbidden to wear, and walk very slowly, as suggestively as we could pull off at that age, past the older guys. If we knew one of them, like he was the brother of a friend or maybe your dad hired him to help with the yard work or shovel the walk, we'd stop to chat for a minute. But just a minute—we had to look casual. On the way back from the ladies, one of the guys he'd been hanging out with usually asked you to dance. If not, you repeated the routine an hour later—eventually, it worked and you got to dance.

"C'mon baby, dance with me!"

Lisa Johnson

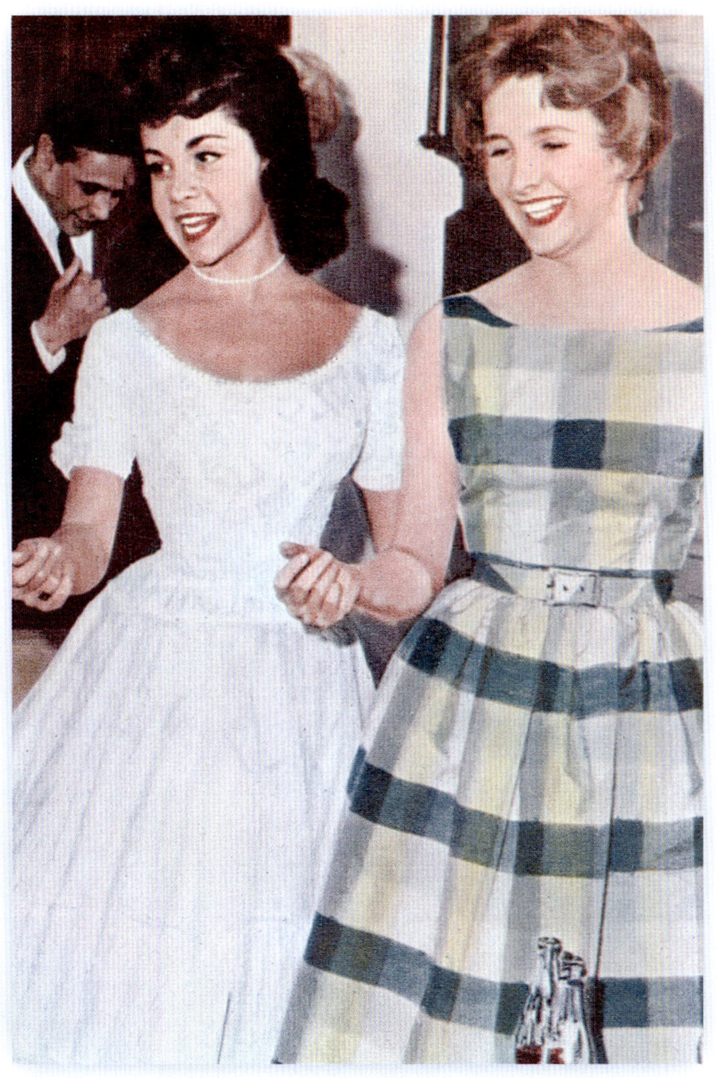

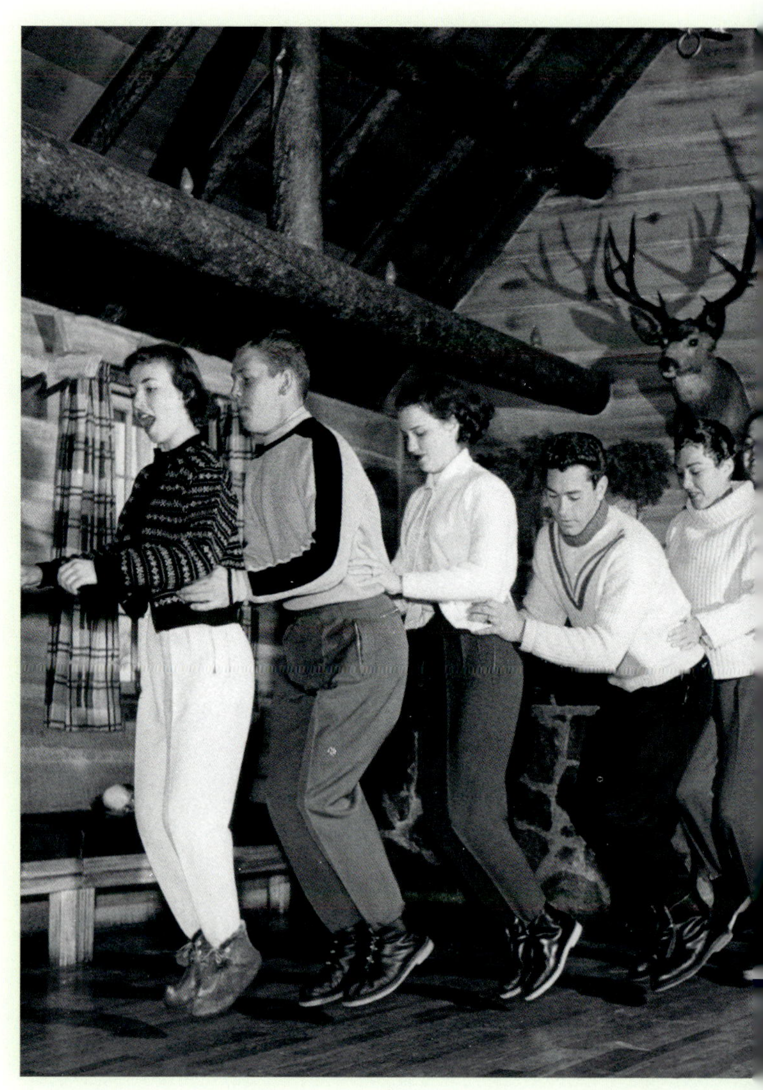

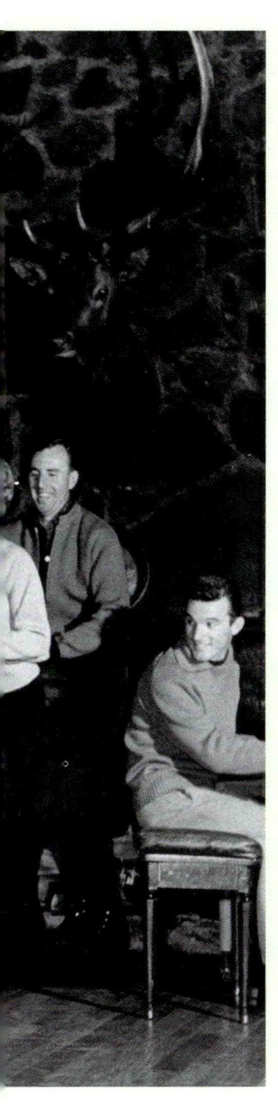

do the bunny hop! hop! hop!

The young dancers on American Bandstand created endless new dances—including the famous bunny hop. Start with right foot forward (heel tap), right foot back (toe tap), then switch feet, putting left foot forward (heel tap), left foot back (toe tap), jump forward (feet together), jump back (feet together), jump (hop), jump (hop), jump (hop).

"Heel/toe—
heel/toe—
forward—back—
hop! hop! hop!"

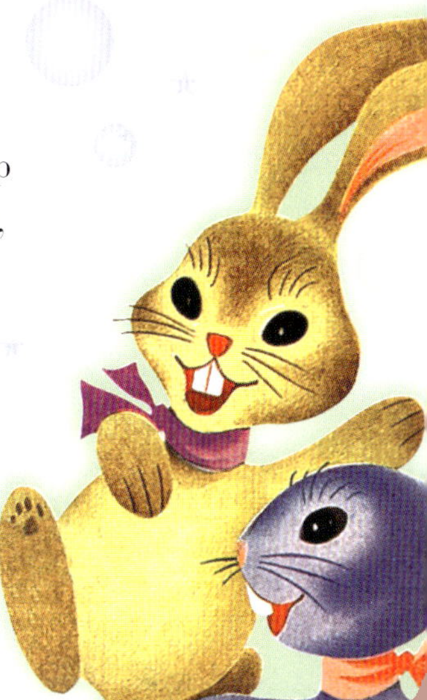

dance crazy!

The Pic-a-Rib Café was a birthplace of my alter ego: the performer. I loved it there because I could be who I wanted to be without schoolteachers' reprimands, parental restrictions, society's expectations, and the narrow moral confinement of the church.

I danced with Ricky and Miss Peggy: loose and cool and uninhibited. It was an era of many dance crazes: the twist, the swim, the

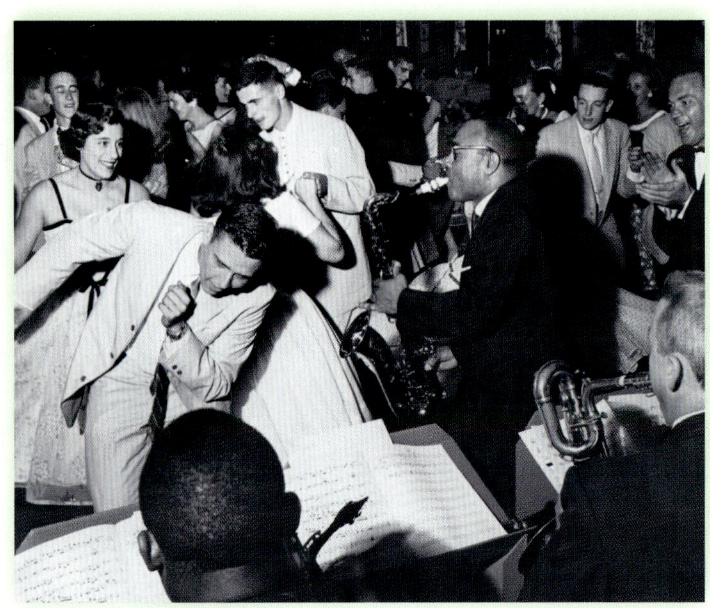

mashed potatoes, pony, continental, fly, Popeye, yo-yo, U.T., bop, jerk, Watutsi, locomotion, monkey, hully gully, hand jive, and a few more I've forgotten.

Carl Gustafson

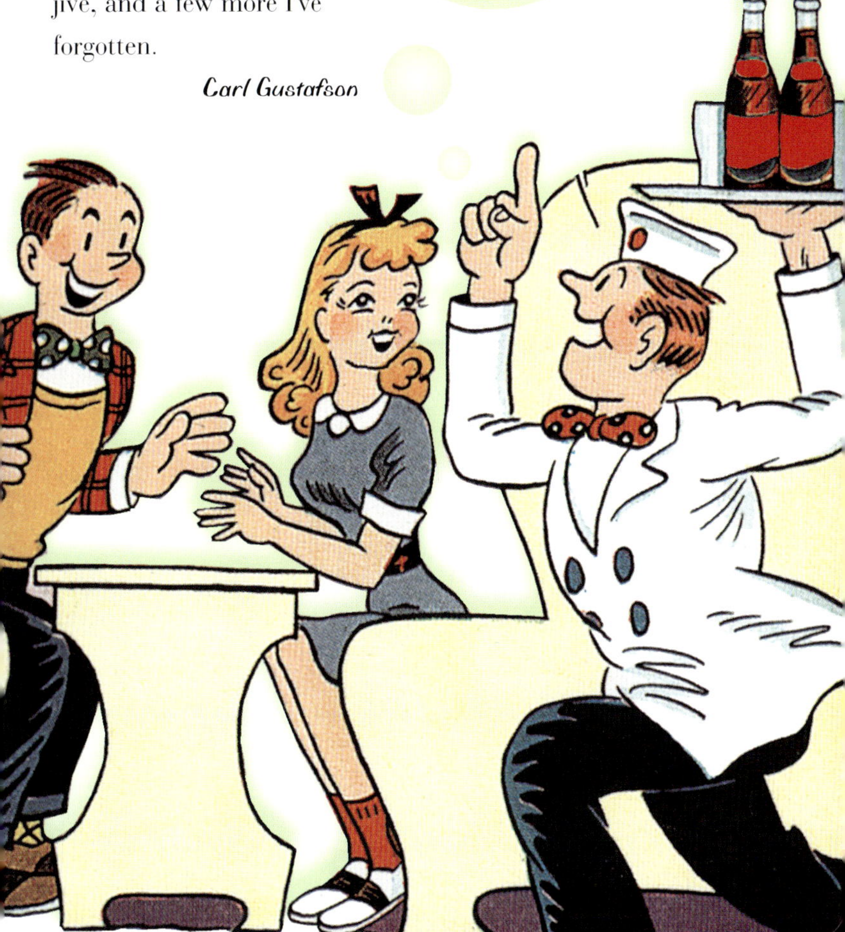

Runaround Sue's Hot Tips for the cutest look ever!

Skirtin' the issue! Hi all you gals. I just love the way my crinoline petticoat holds my skirt out—it makes my waist look so cute and tiny—I feel like I'm queen of the hop. Now I've found a hot tip to keep it just like new. Here's what to do!

After washing your petticoat, put it in a dishpan filled with starch. While it's absorbing all the starch, find the biggest umbrella in the house. Take it outside, open it up and stick the handle in the ground. Now get some clothespins. Take your dishpan outside and drape your petticoat over the umbrella. Use the clothespins to attach it all around. When it's dry, it'll be just like you bought it from the store! Coolsville!

yakkety yak!

Going straight? Now I know, girls, how many of you are getting those crazy, new, straight skirts. They are the coolest—especially when you pair them with a nice pair of saddles and some sparkling white rolled socks. But the problem is—well, you've seen it

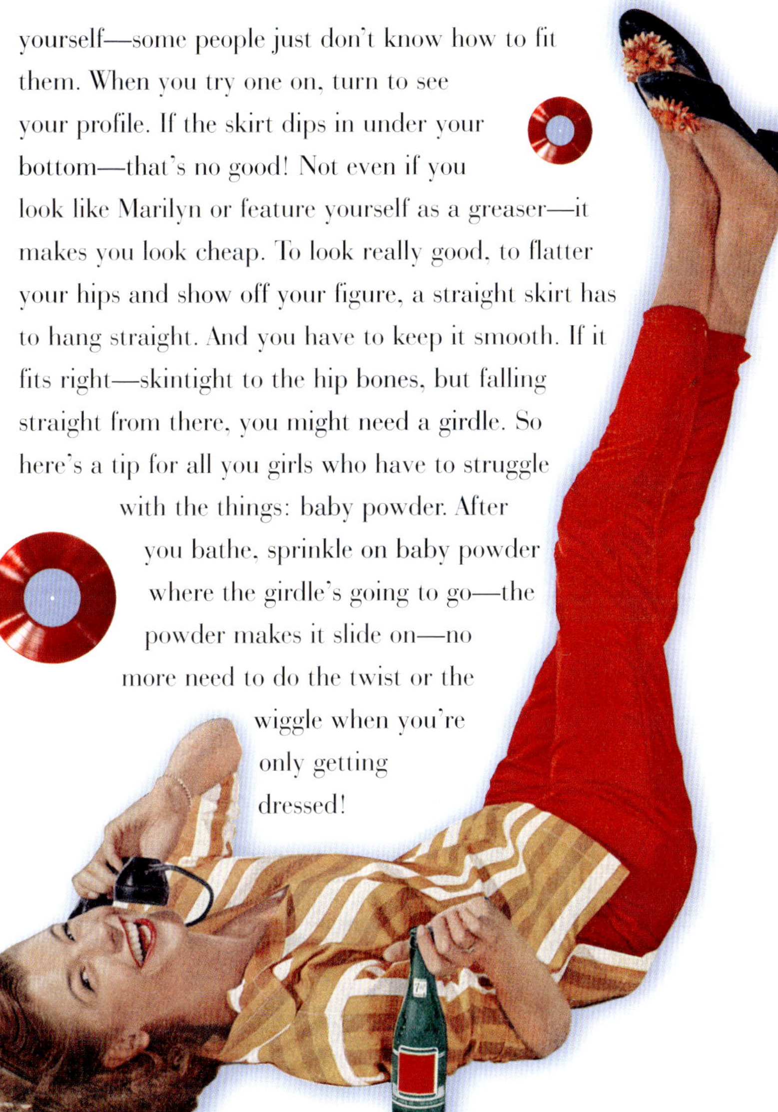

yourself—some people just don't know how to fit them. When you try one on, turn to see your profile. If the skirt dips in under your bottom—that's no good! Not even if you look like Marilyn or feature yourself as a greaser—it makes you look cheap. To look really good, to flatter your hips and show off your figure, a straight skirt has to hang straight. And you have to keep it smooth. If it fits right—skintight to the hip bones, but falling straight from there, you might need a girdle. So here's a tip for all you girls who have to struggle with the things: baby powder. After you bathe, sprinkle on baby powder where the girdle's going to go—the powder makes it slide on—no more need to do the twist or the wiggle when you're only getting dressed!

learning from TV

Marty Robbins sang "A White Sport Coat" and the Searchers came out with a new song that started a new dance step—the stroll. We learned the new crazes in dance by watching Dick Clark host the American Bandstand.

Reba and J.B. Criner

"Where's my pink carnation?"

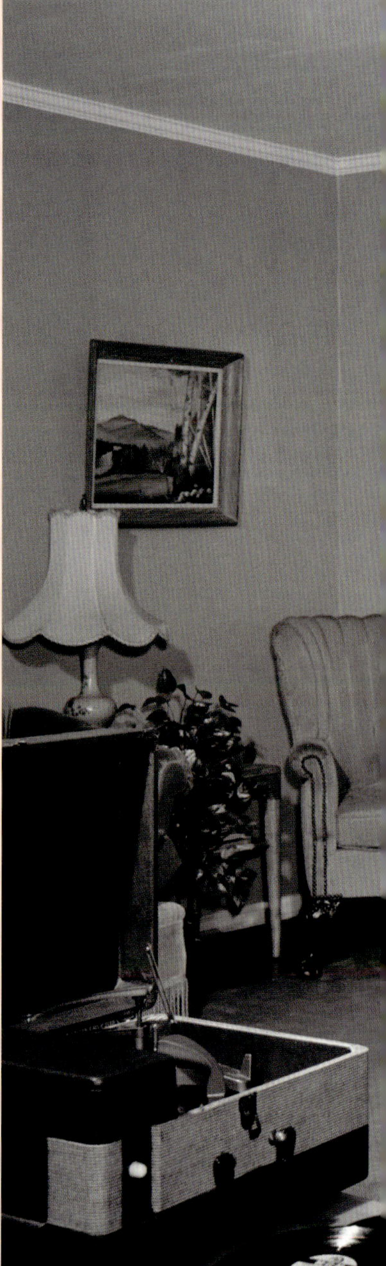

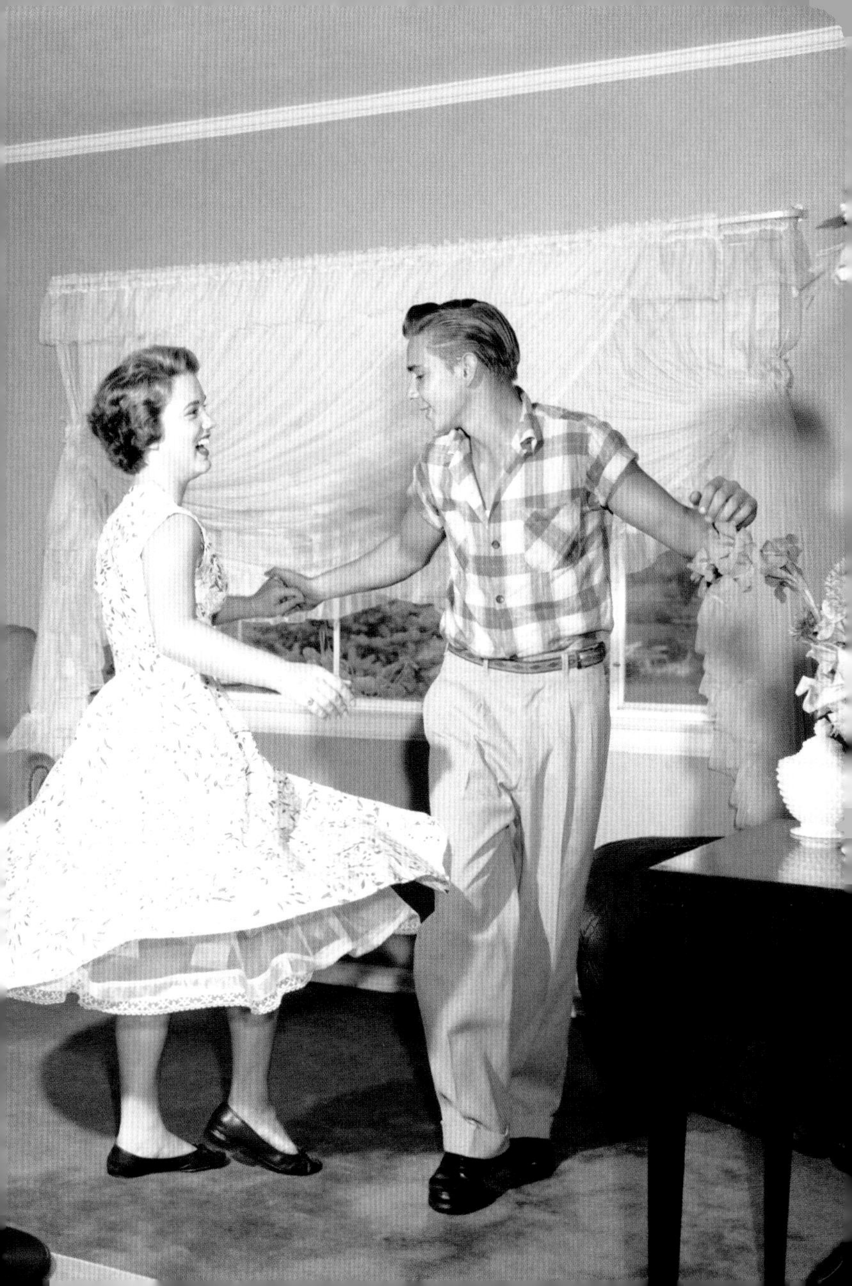

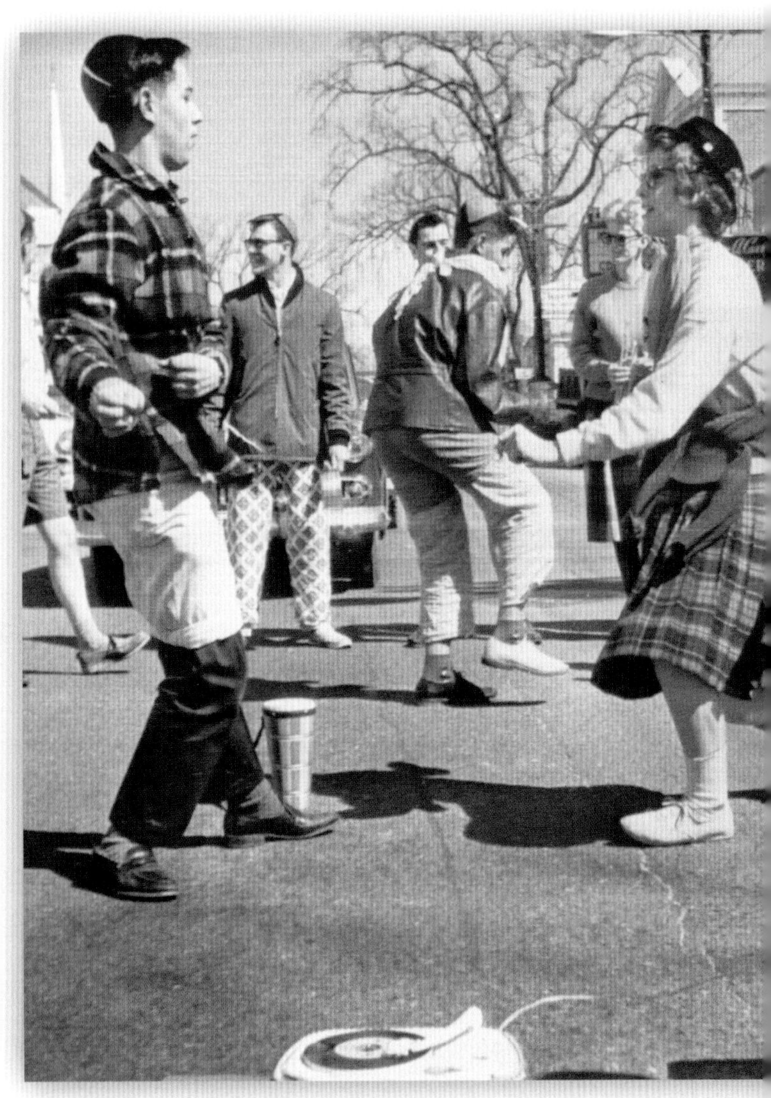

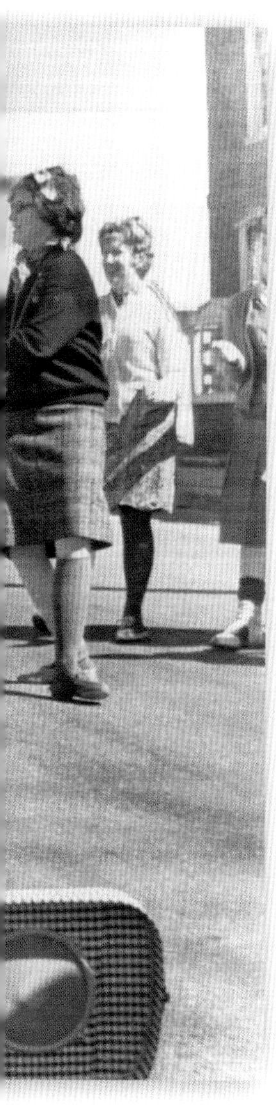

let's twist again!

Chubby Checker launched the twist on Dick Clark's Bandstand and revolutionized teen dancing! Everyone was doing the twist. Try it! it goes like this: stand with one leg set forward slightly, then slowly start twisting your hips. Now speed up until you're in sync with the music—but remember, you have to make it look smooth. Do long, continuous, movements, not jerks. Once you've got the general idea, you can get more adventurous: twist right down to a crouch, and then twist back upright again. Don't cheat—to do this properly, you must continue twisting all the way down and back up again! And if you're really cool, try twisting while bending backward as far as you can!

"Come on everybody, clap your hands!"

Chapter 2

ROCK AROUND THE CLOCK

Bill Haley's "Rock Around the Clock" hit the charts in 1955; the following year, Elvis released "Heartbreak Hotel." But they were just two in a galaxy of stars including Buddy Holly, Roy Orbison, Ricky Nelson, Eddie Cochrane, the Everly Brothers, Fabian, Johnny Mathis and Pat Boone. Fans listened to Alan Freeman's radio show, and tuned in to WLAC in Nashville for hits by black doo-wop heroes such as Chuck Berry, who inspired rock and roll.

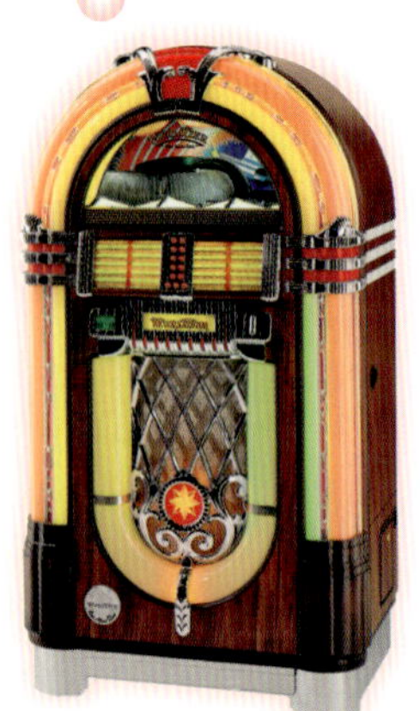

Rock and roll is an economic thing. Today's nine-to-fourteen-year-old group is the first generation with enough money given to them by their parents to buy records in sufficient quantities to influence the market.

Singer Jo Stafford,
quoted in Billboard, October 13, 1958

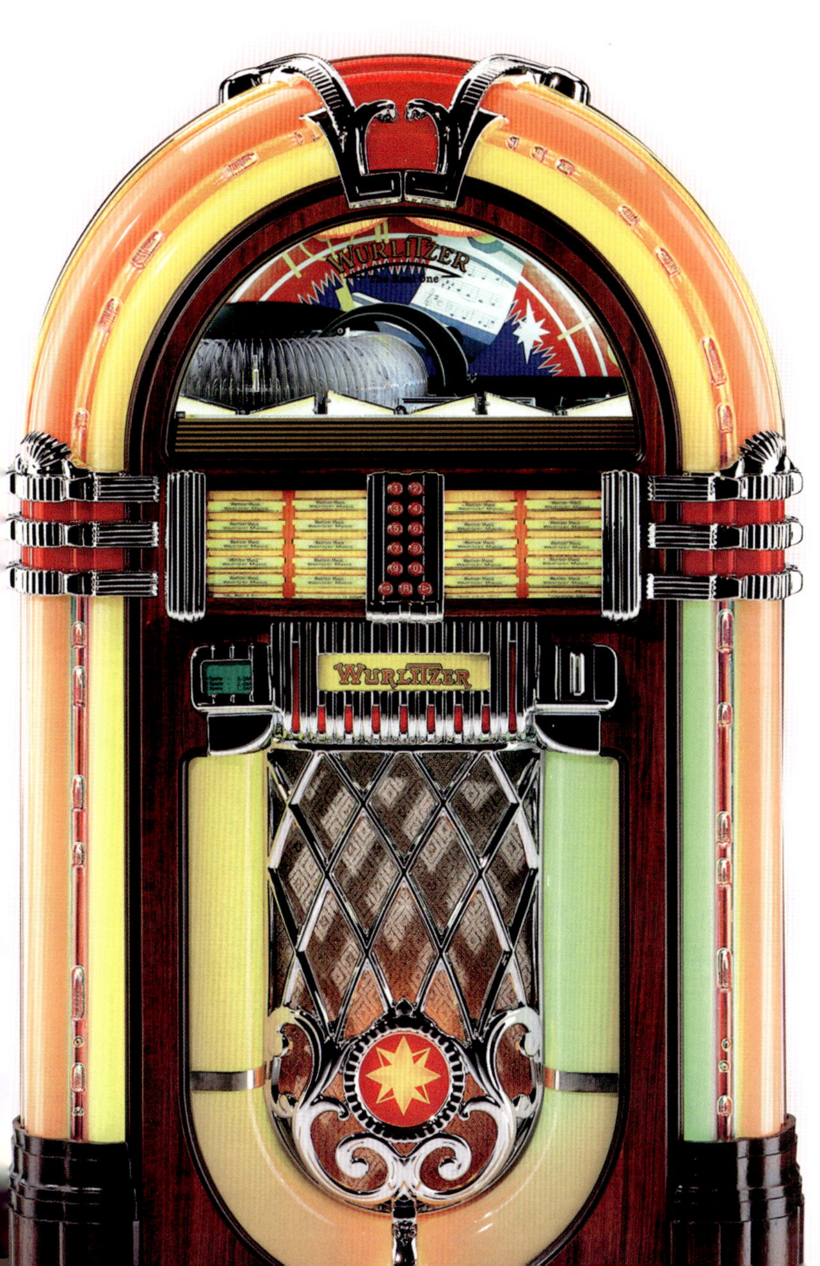
WURLITZER
WURLITZER

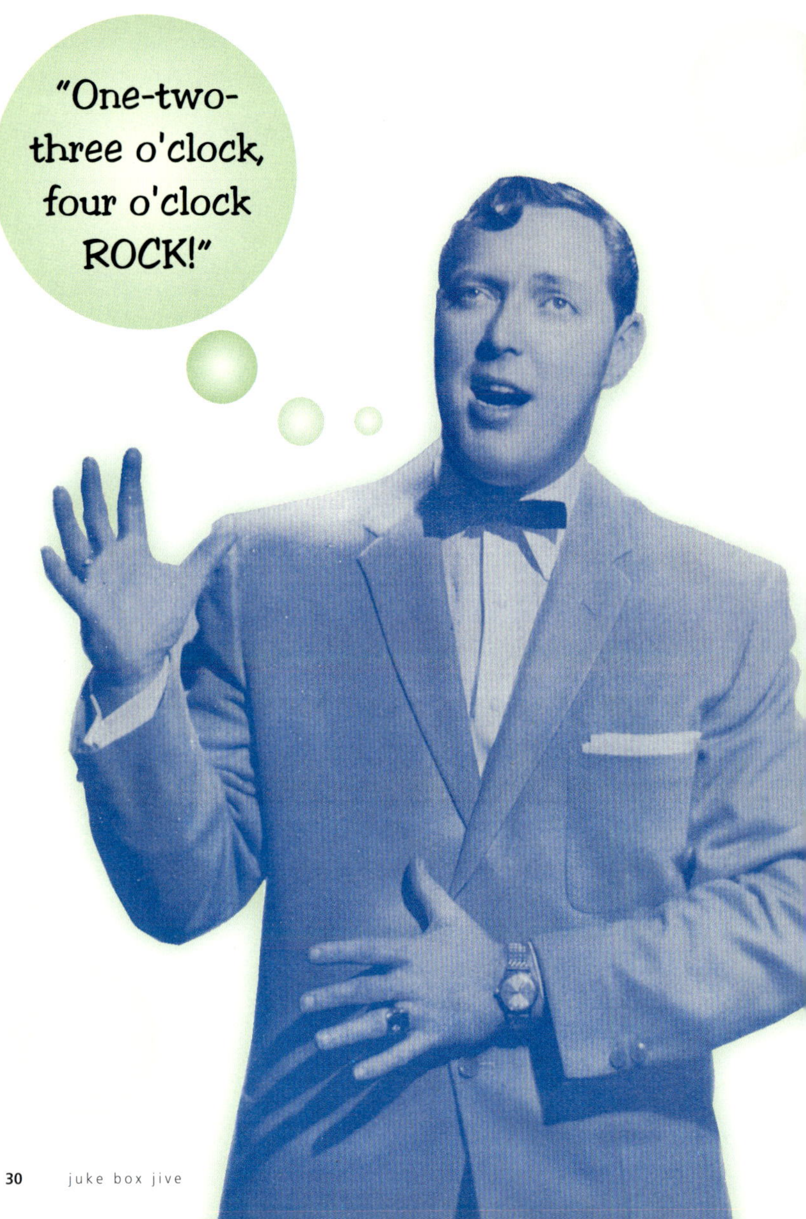
"One-two-
three o'clock,
four o'clock
ROCK!"

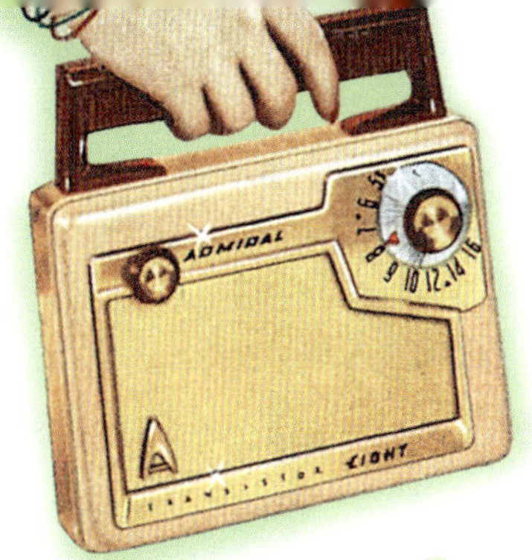

Bill Haley? Well, of course! I mean, just about everyone who was around in the '50s remembers the first time they heard "Rock Around the Clock." You knew at once that it was something special. It sounded different. It felt different. It was different. You just had to get up and dance to that tune—we all went wild. My brother and his girlfriend were great sock hop dancers—they jived to it all the time. I always think of the thrill "Rock Around the Clock" gave us—for me it was the anthem of rock and roll.

Rita Murphy

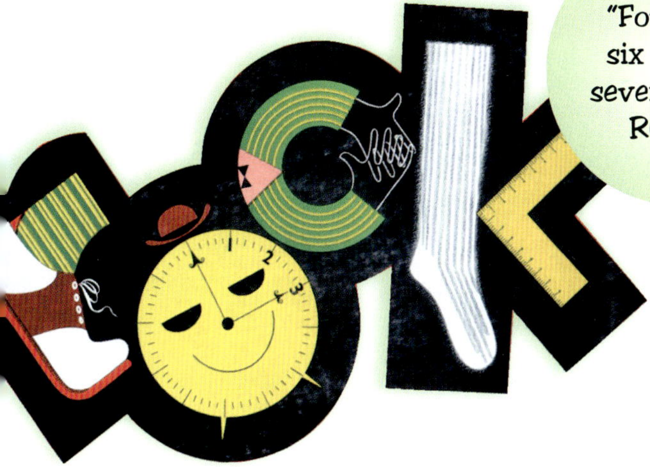

"Four-five-six o'clock, seven o'clock ROCK!"

Chuck Berry—our doo-wop hero!

At night, we'd listen to WLAC, out of Nashville. I was in Pittsburgh, but the whole east coast could get it, and the whole east coast listened to it. It was doo-wop—black music. We guys didn't listen to the white music—that was for the kids in the suburbs. We thought Pat Boone was toxic. If you were working class, growing up in the poor part of a city, you listened to black music. That's what you identified with. We hated Elvis when he appeared. He was a pretender, an imitation, and he dominated everything. No way, man. The music we listened to was Chuck Berry, Jimmy Reed, Lowell Fulson, Lightning Hopkins, Muddy Waters, Little Junior Parker, the Spaniels, Sonny Boy Williamson, Howling Wolf, and Etta James. They were the greats.

"Go, Johnny go, go-go, Johnny B. Good!"

Tom Lowell

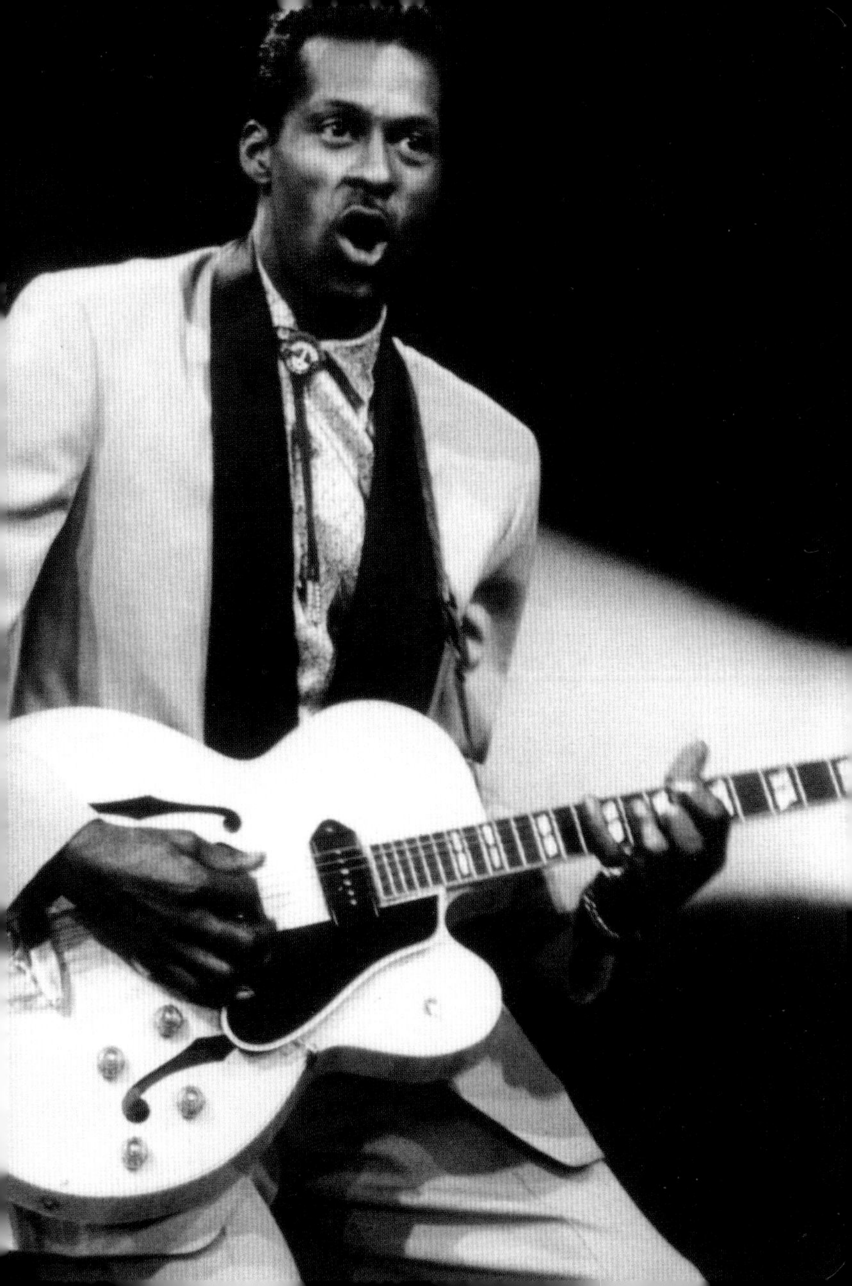

clean-cut family man

Pat Boone really was something else. I mean, when you come to think about it, it was just like he was waiting around for Little Richard to come up with his next hit. Then, sure enough, Pat would be out there with his own version. It got to be quite funny—I mean which "Tutti-Frutti" would you be buying—his or Little Richard's? In my book, there was no contest. I went for Little Richard every time. The thing was, Pat Boone could really sing. But he came over as the clean-cut family man, and I guess that's what he thought would get him his own audience. And it did. Some people idolized him. He even had his own magazine for teens.

Meg Sutton

"When you get married you forget abou kissing other women."

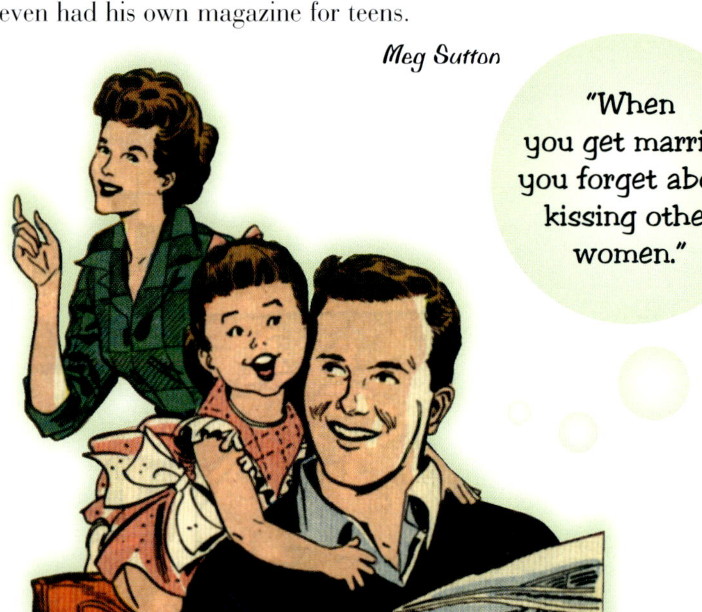

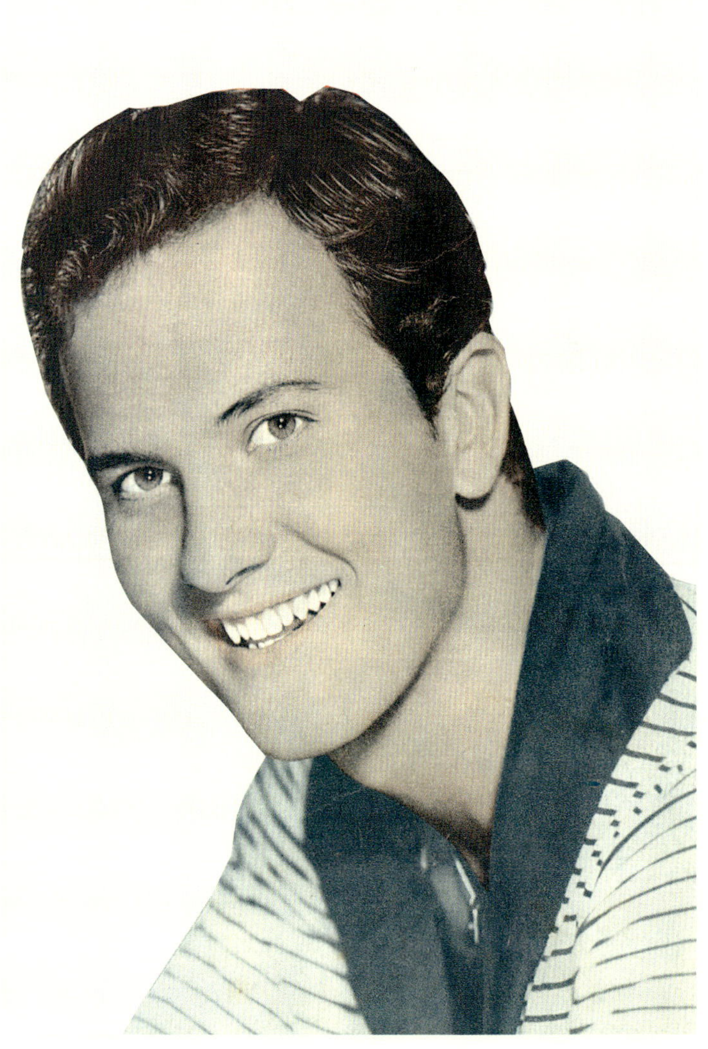

where the boys are...

Connie Francis? We all liked "Who's Sorry Now" and "Stupid Cupid." She was one of those girl singers who had this "cute" appeal—you know, there was her, Doris Day and Connie Stevens—they were all going for that sort of image—the pert, pretty look.

Jaynie Allen

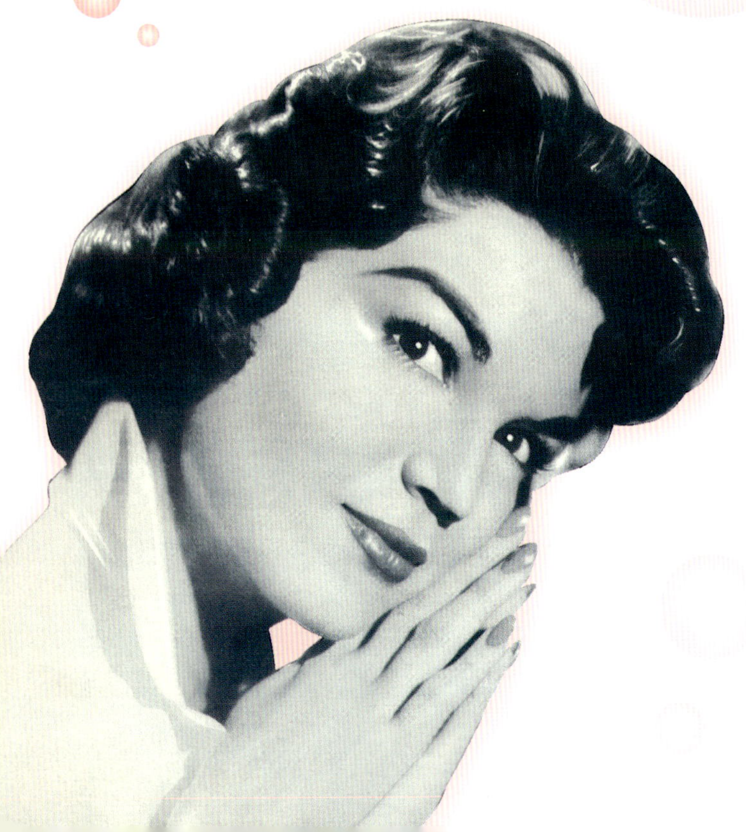

"Connie adores amusement parks, foreign accents, roller skating, "brainy" people, speed, Broadway after dark, babies' toes and collecting stuffed animals (she has 44). She dislikes calories, boastful men, insects and lightning. She hides in her closet during thunderstorms!"

Pat Boone Magazine, 1960

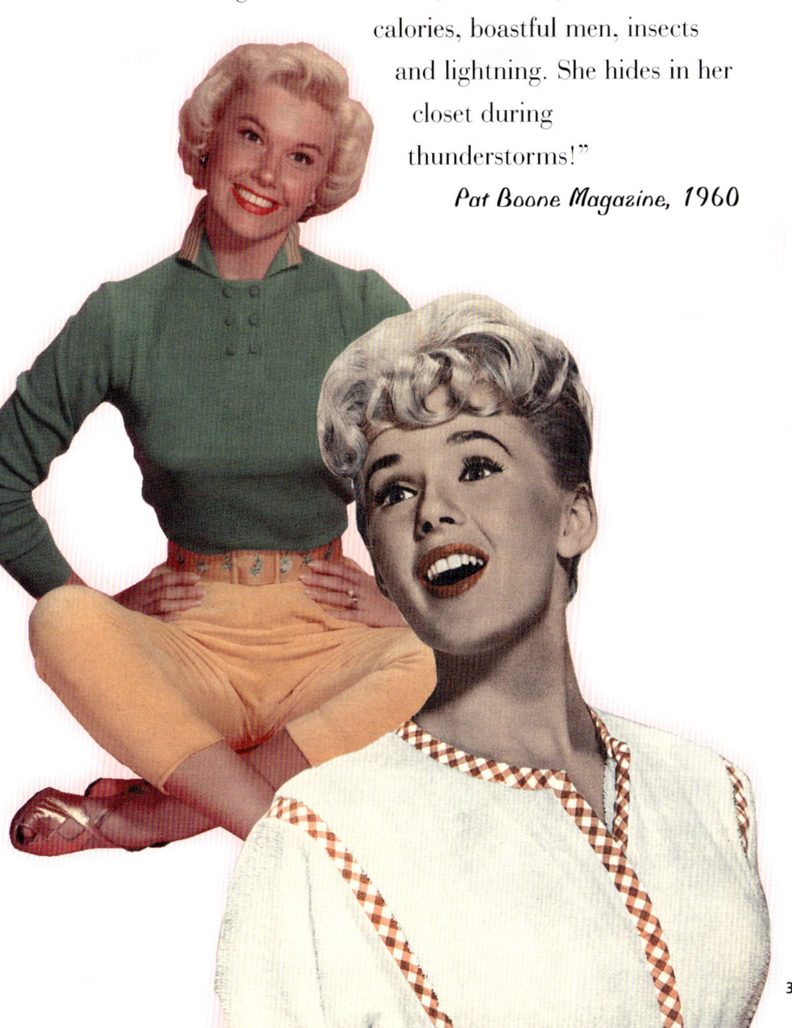

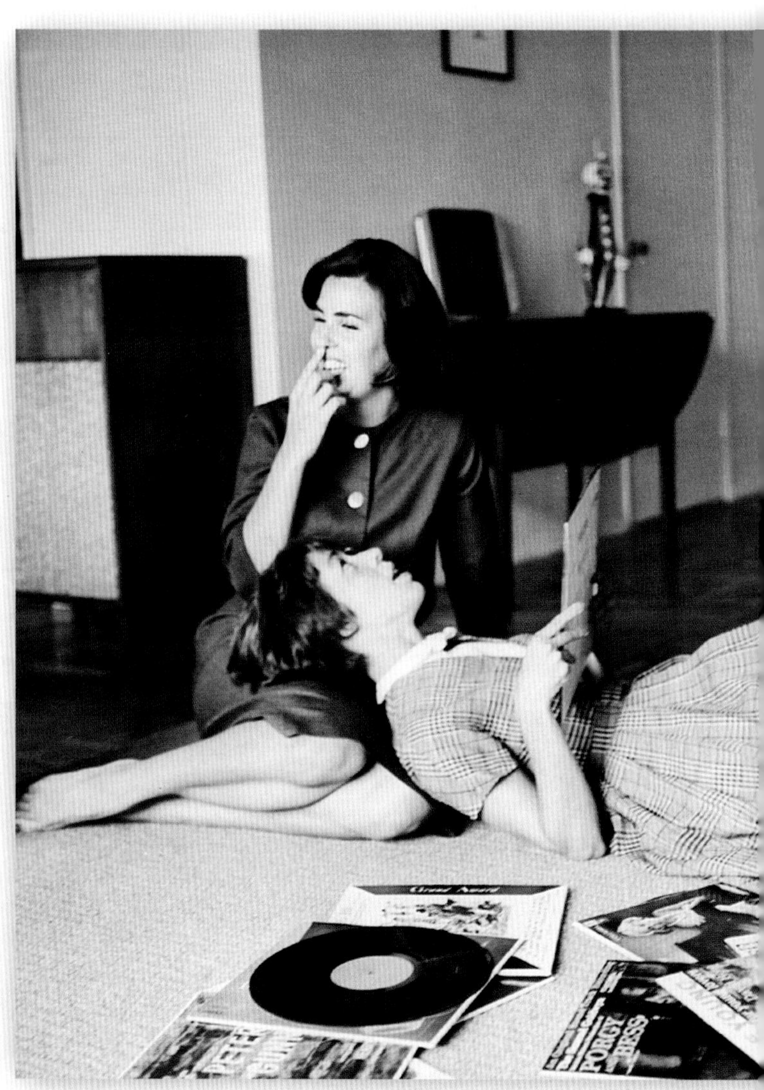
PORGY
BESS

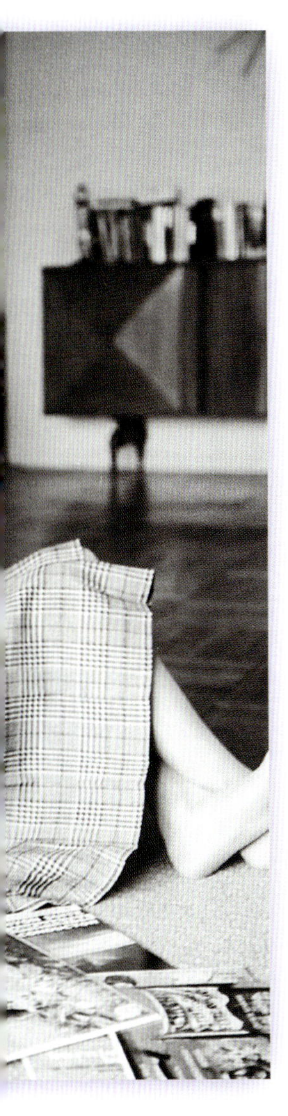

those dreamy heartthrobs

I'm sure my mother used to dread my slumber parties because it was me and a bunch of my friends playing endless records, one after the other. But truly, what great songs they were! We liked the sad, tragic, mushy ones best—Paul Anka singing "Diana"; Johnny Mathis and his "Twelfth of Never"; and, of course, anything by the Everly Brothers. "Devoted to you" was my favorite. We knew all the words, and sang along. And we'd cry real tears. Then we'd laugh at each other.

Cindy Morrison

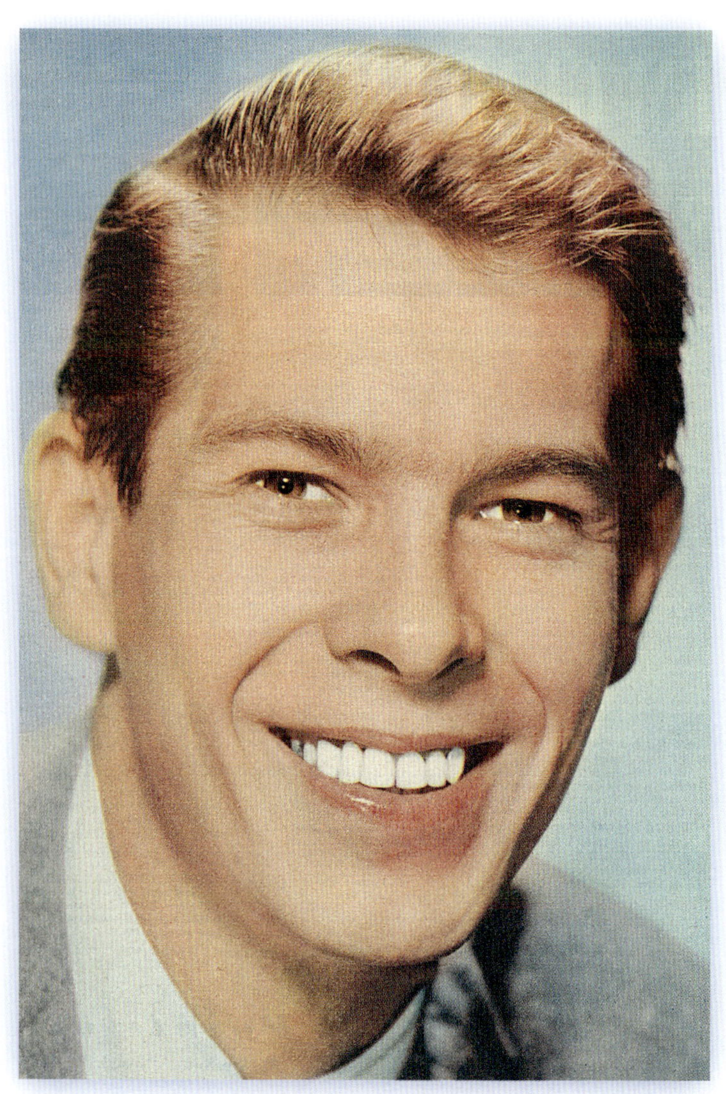

cry! cry! cry!

Johnny Ray was the first guy I ever saw who was totally emotional on stage—he threw himself into his performances in a way I'd never seen before. It was exciting. He would somehow contort his entire body, and his face was full of pain. He had two big hits that I remember very well—they were really sad songs called "Cry" and "The Little White Cloud that Cried." We listened to them a lot. I think they were on the same album, because we just turned it straight over. And, of course, we loved all that sad stuff because we were typical teenagers. I never did get to go to any of his concerts, but we knew about all the girls in the audiences screaming and sobbing. What did they call him? The "Nabob of Sob!"—something like that.

Louise R. Franks

Johnny Ray—we called him Mr. Emotion!

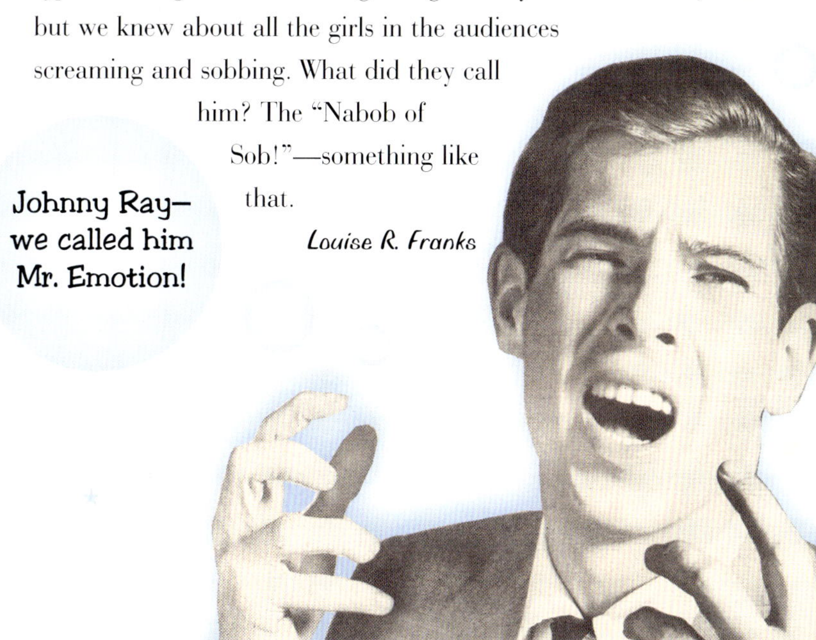

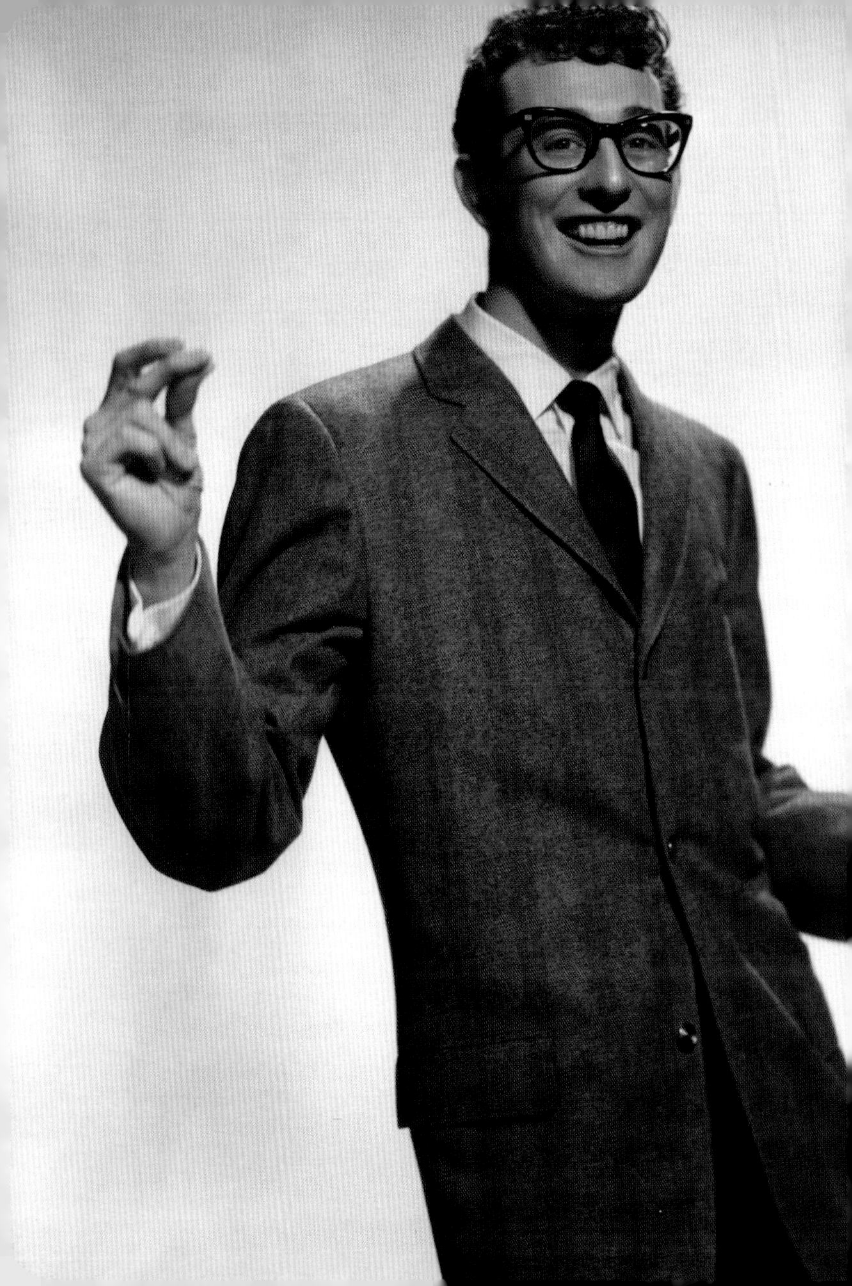

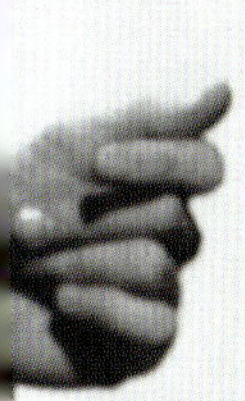

something deeper

Buddy Holly was the first and last person that the famous singer Don Mclean completely idolized when he was a kid. Most of his friends liked Elvis Presley more than Holly. But Don was hooked. As he said, "I liked Holly because he spoke to me. He was a symbol of something deeper than the music he made."

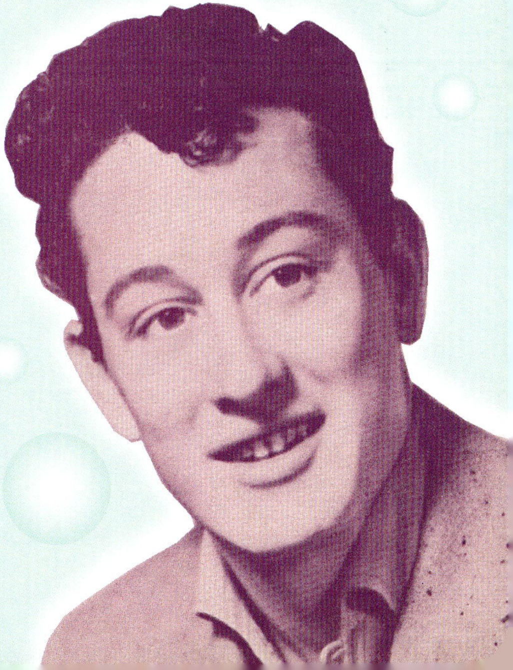

jukebox Saturday night

At King's X, a block or two south of the Dairy Queen on Oliver Street in the eastern part of Wichita, we'd go inside and sit at tables with booths and tops that in later years were Formica with boomerangs, and a jukebox menu of songs that played Buddy Holly and Ricky Nelson and all the standards. And my sister and I would flip through the pages to read the titles and singers.

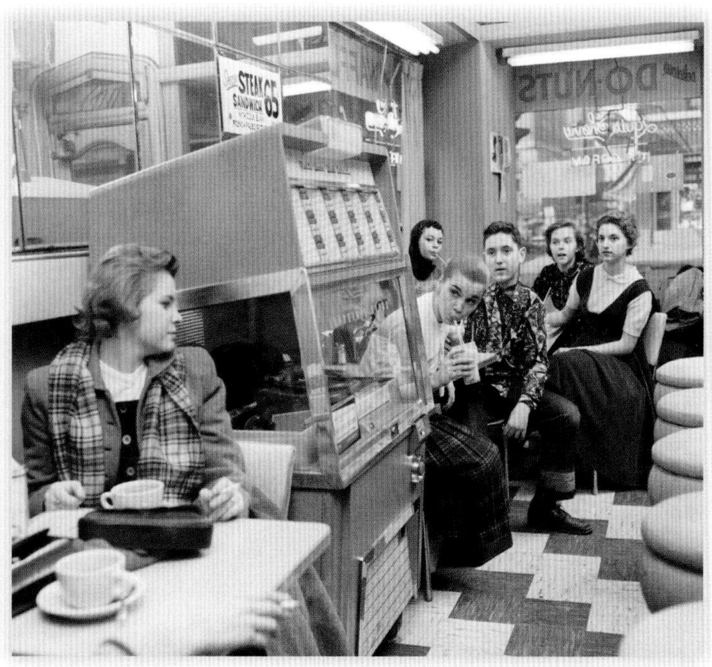

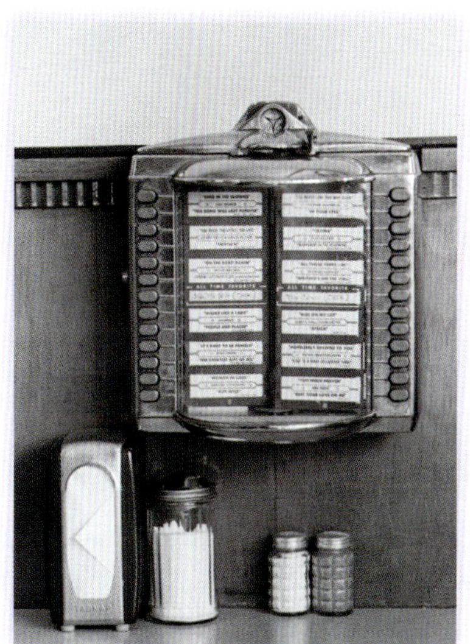

The real records that got played were in an actual jukebox, but there was a tabletop record selector with a coin slot and bright red buttons in two rows along the bottom front, and menus of songs, about six per page, that opened up like pages in a book only they were stiff and operated by sliding a hook in the top along a curved track, one per page, and then you'd put in some money and choose a song, like D-8, and when it was your turn, that song would play. Only we didn't have money for that, so we just looked.

Rod Owen

"Without preamble, the three-piece band cuts loose. In the spotlight, the lanky singer flails furious rhythms on his guitar, every now and then breaking a string. In a pivoting stance, his hips swing sensuously from side to side and his entire body takes on a frantic quiver, as if he had swallowed a jackhammer."

Time Magazine, May 15, 1956

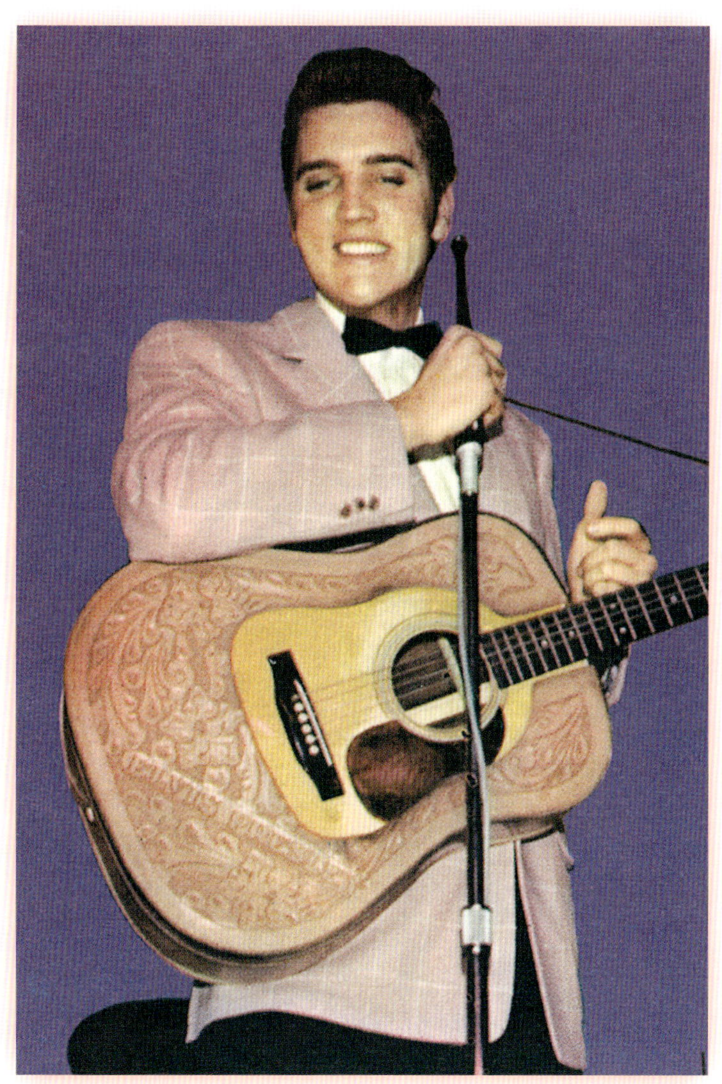

I'm not trying to be sexy...

I never heard more than a few words of any song clearly. Elvis had only to lift an eyebrow or hitch up his pants and whatever he was singing was lost in the screaming of the mob. No one was interested in hearing him sing or play. One reporter said: "If it had been anyone else, the police would have closed the show in ten minutes!" "He's the cutest, sweetest entertainer there ever was. They're not being fair to him just because his style is different," pleaded a typical teenage fan, upset at a typical attack on her teenage idol.

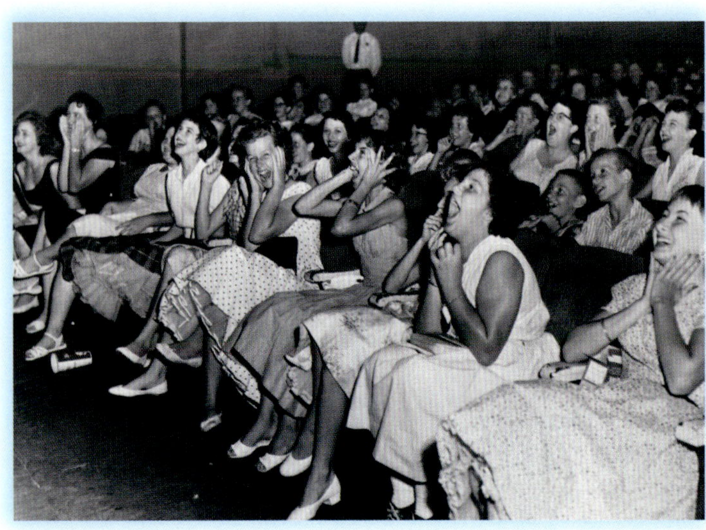

Elvis himself was deeply disturbed by the uproar. In his own defense: "Man, when I sing I go into a complete trance from which I don't come out at all. Why, if I couldn't dance when I sing, I wouldn't be living. I'm not trying to be sexy, I just feel that rhythm and I'm sent."

Movie Stars Parade, 1958

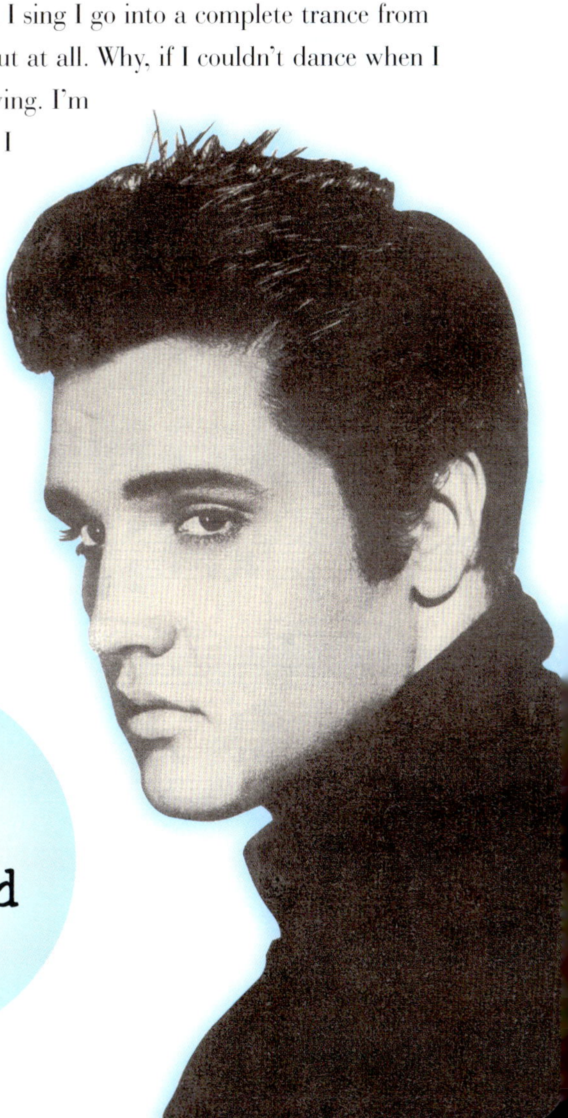

...I just feel that rhythm and I'm sent.

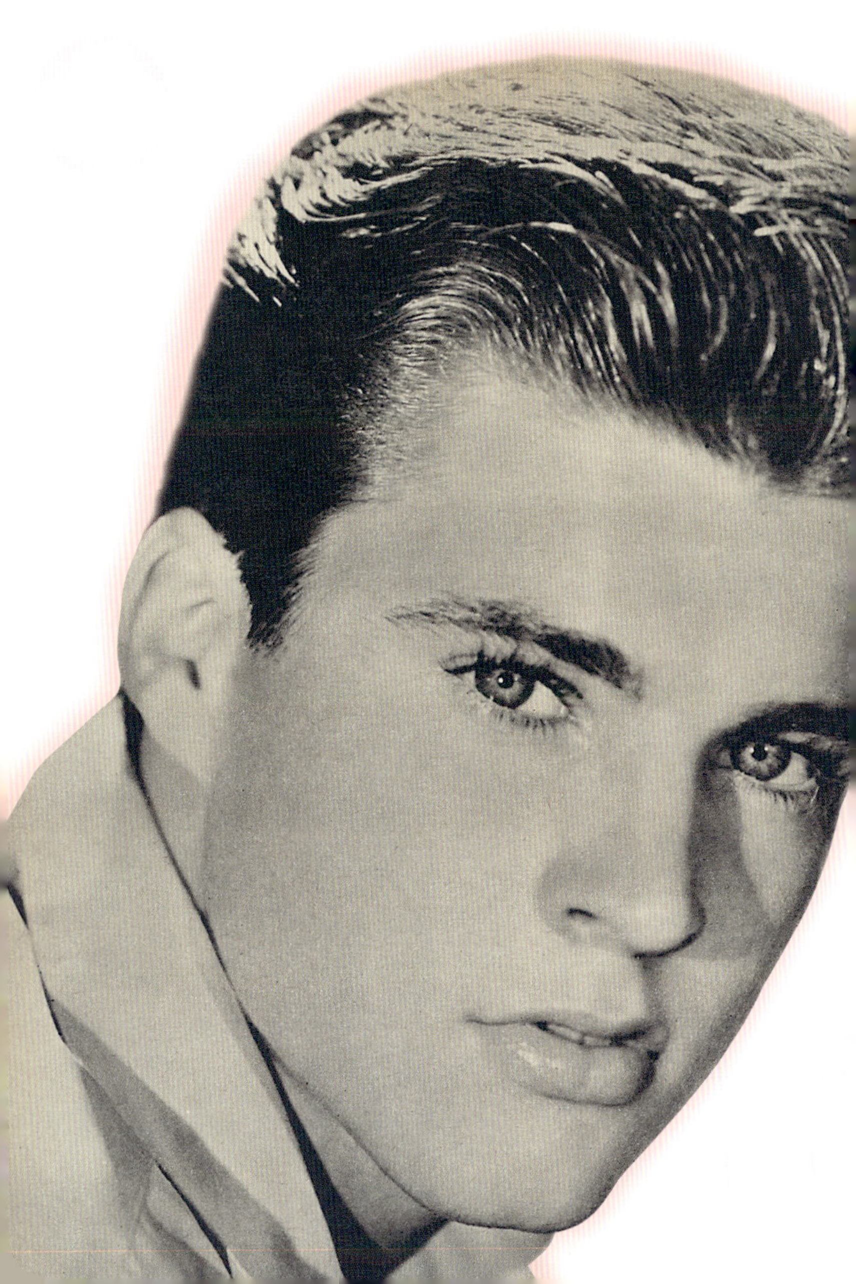

I only know two cats in this business that really had it all; Elvis was one of those guys, the other was Ricky Nelson. There was a difference in those two guys, though. Elvis moved…Ricky never had to; he stood flat footed and captivated his audience with his good looks. We grew up with him; those who didn't missed something. History books are gonna have to say that he played a big role in rock'n roll music…he did it his way.

Carl Perkins

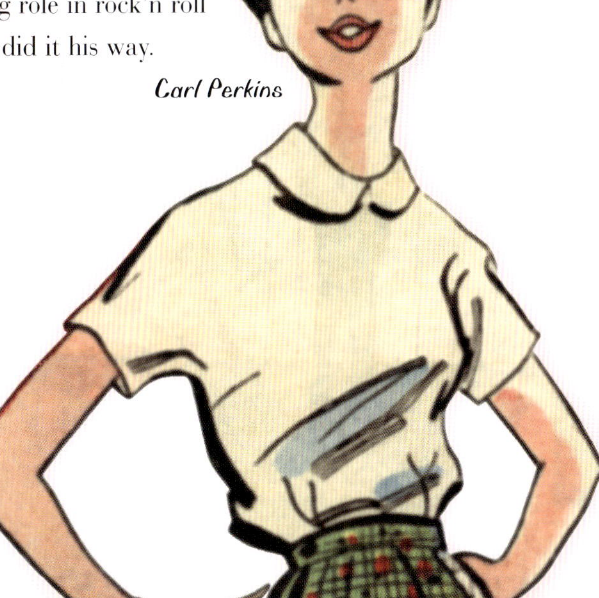

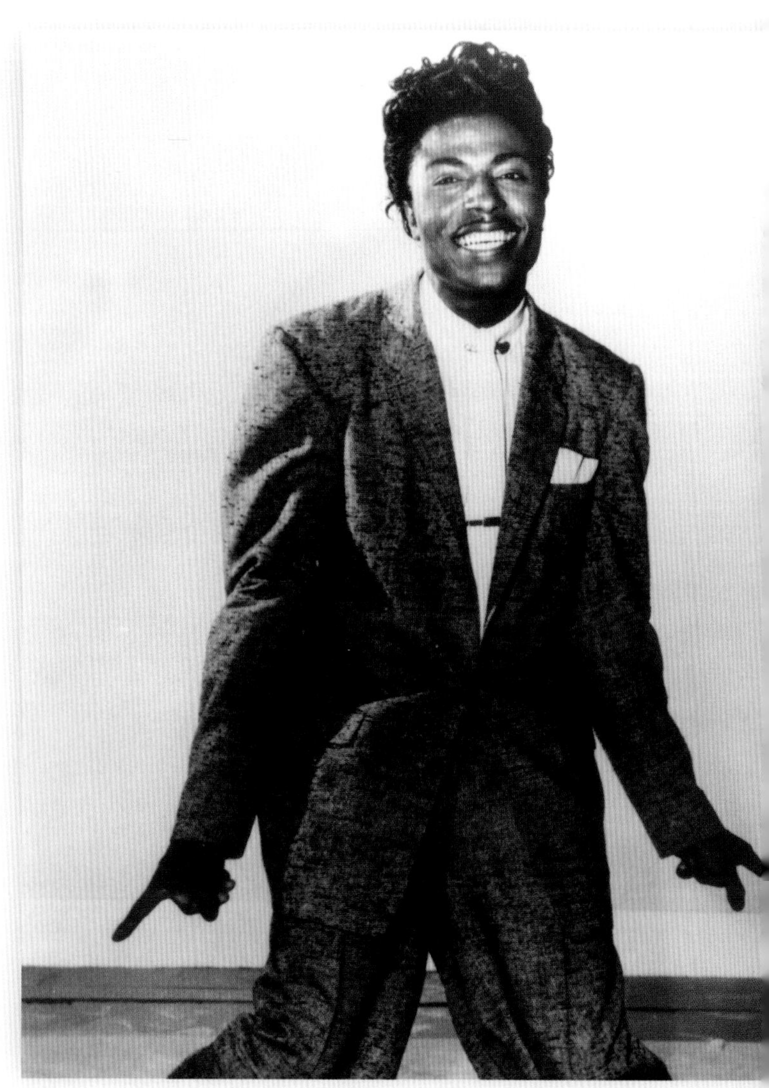

those immortal lines

A wild black man known as Little Richard soon arrived on the scene with a rasping voice and frantic piano style. Many of his rock'n'roll numbers were self-penned, a new innovation in popular music, and they were nearly all sung at a frantic pace, and included crazy and often nonsensical lyrics. Richard Penniman gave the world those immortal lines: "A-wop-bam-a-looma-a-wop-bam-boom," and a host of rock'n'roll standards like "Good Golly Miss Molly," "Long Tall Sally," etc.

Tony Papard

"A-wop-
bam-a-looma-
a-wop-bam-
boom!"

payola scandal

The record industry was a huge money spinner during the 1950s, and soon became mired in bribery scandals. Accusations of "payola" were even leveled against Dick Clark, clean-cut presenter of American Bandstand, the top TV music and dance show. Singing idol Fabian spoke out in Clark's defense:

"Dick is the country's top disc jockey," said Fabian. "He can write his own ticket wherever he goes. A man in a position like that doesn't need the small change end of the business, the payola stuff. And anyone that knows Dick will bear that out. Just ask them."

What does Dick Clark say? "I never took payola."

Movie TV Secrets, April 1959

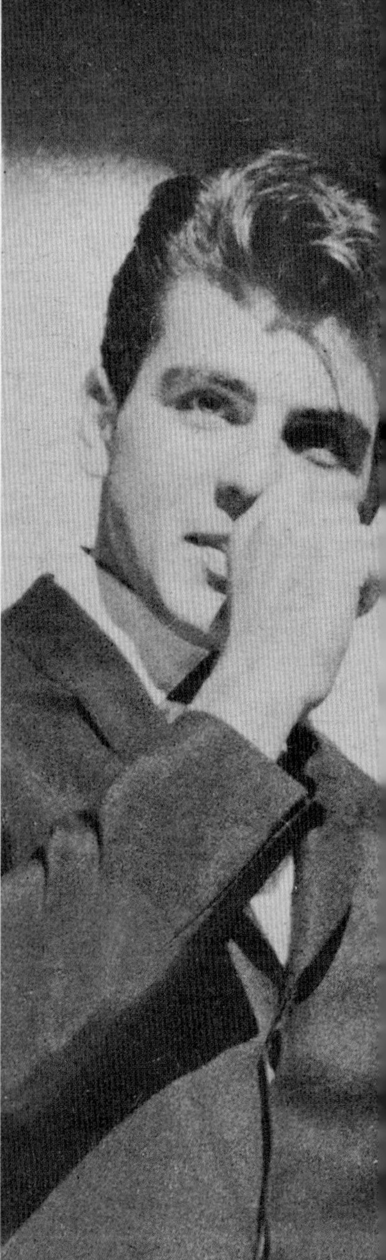

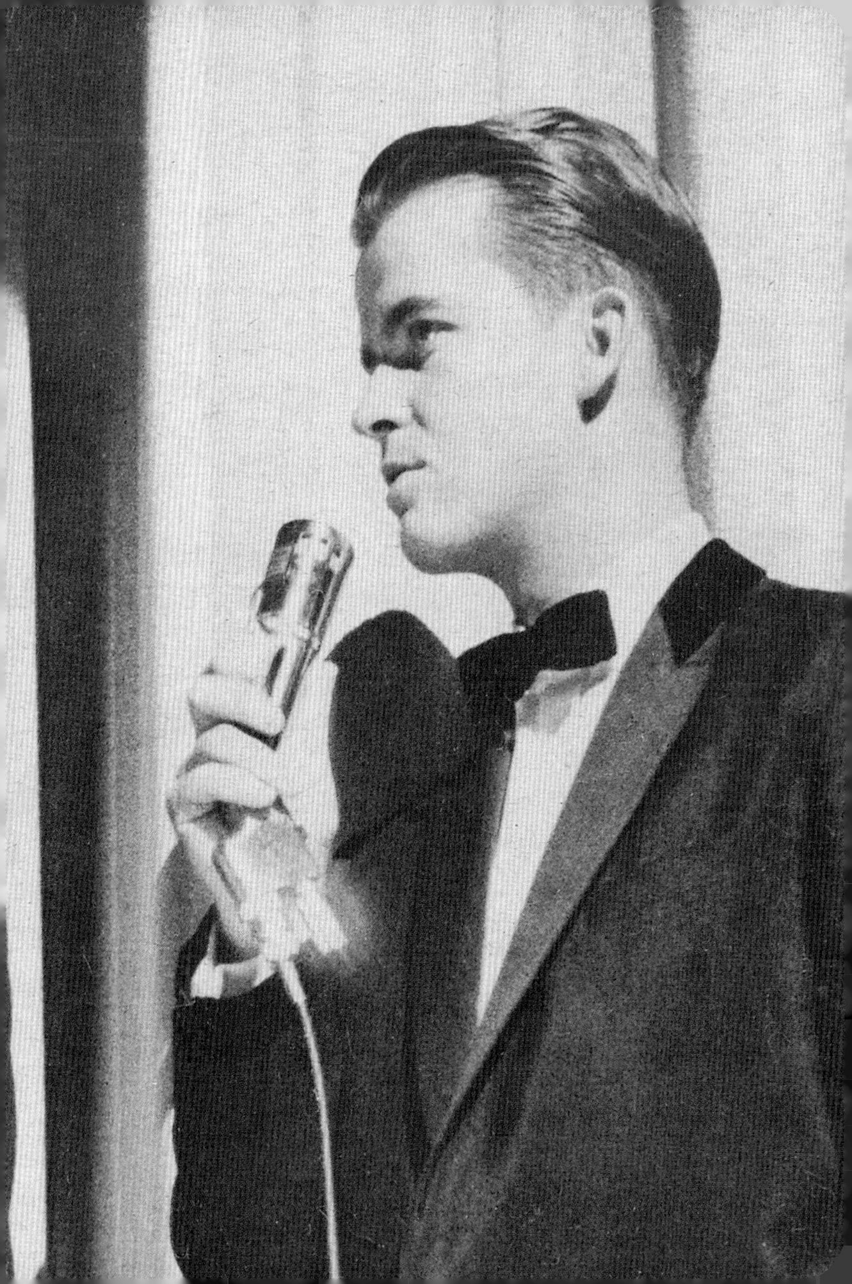

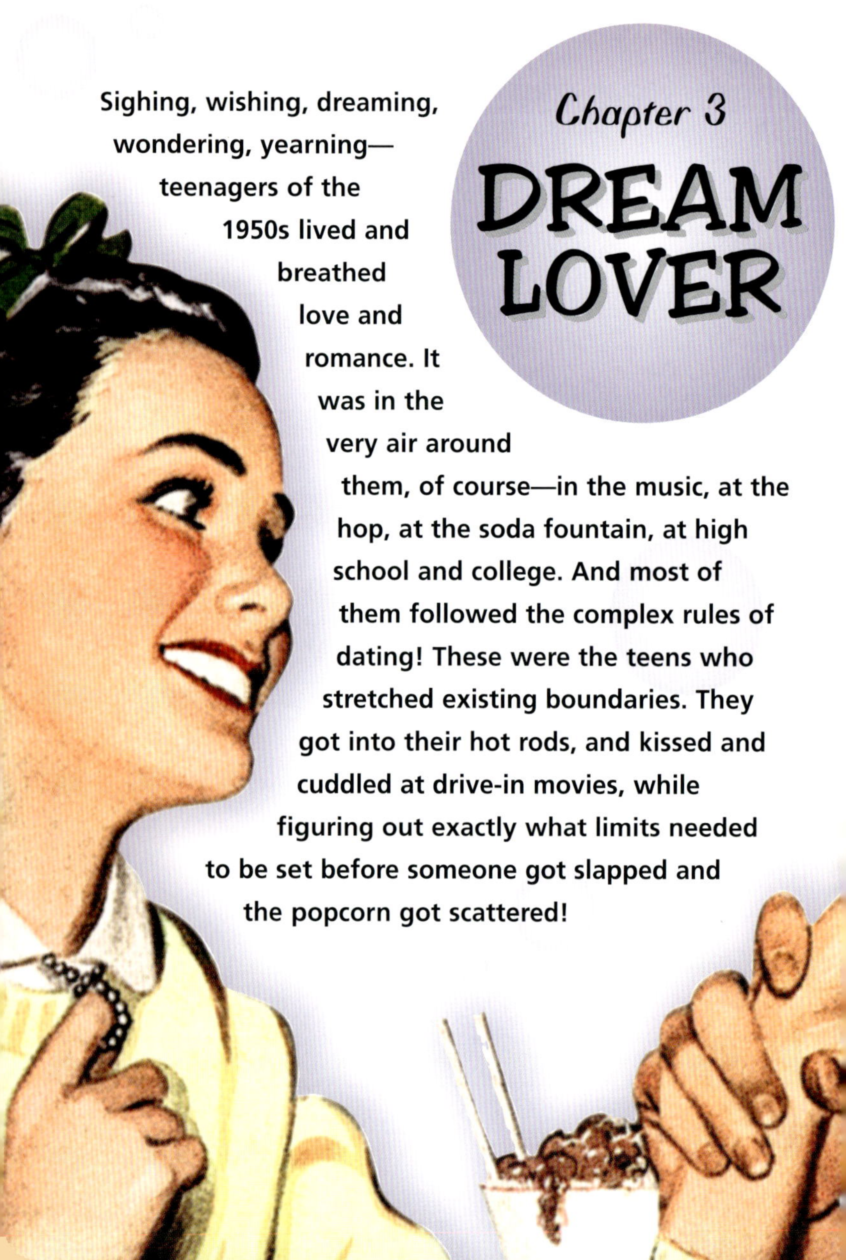

Chapter 3

DREAM LOVER

Sighing, wishing, dreaming, wondering, yearning—teenagers of the 1950s lived and breathed love and romance. It was in the very air around them, of course—in the music, at the hop, at the soda fountain, at high school and college. And most of them followed the complex rules of dating! These were the teens who stretched existing boundaries. They got into their hot rods, and kissed and cuddled at drive-in movies, while figuring out exactly what limits needed to be set before someone got slapped and the popcorn got scattered!

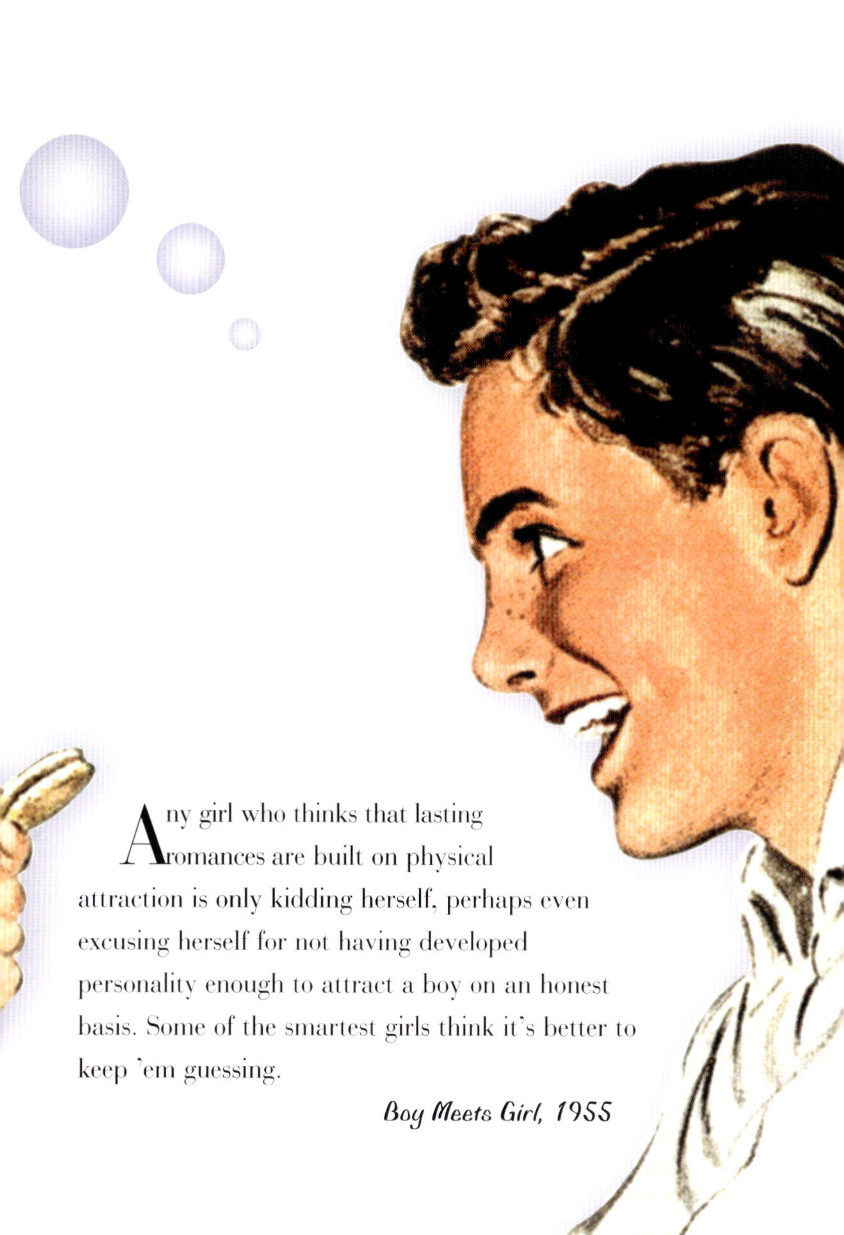

Any girl who thinks that lasting romances are built on physical attraction is only kidding herself, perhaps even excusing herself for not having developed personality enough to attract a boy on an honest basis. Some of the smartest girls think it's better to keep 'em guessing.

Boy Meets Girl, 1955

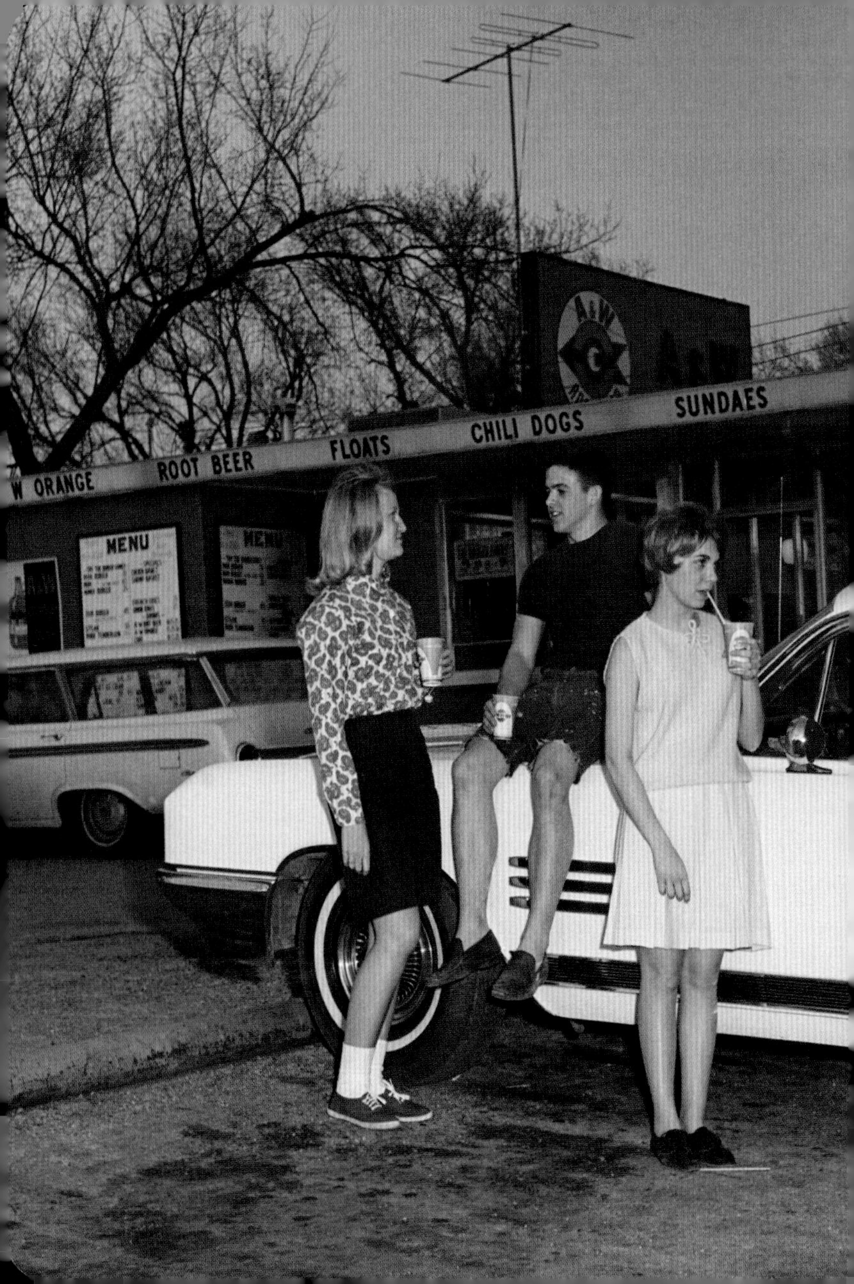
ORANGE
ROOT BEER
FLOATS
CHILI DOGS
SUNDAES
MENU
MENU

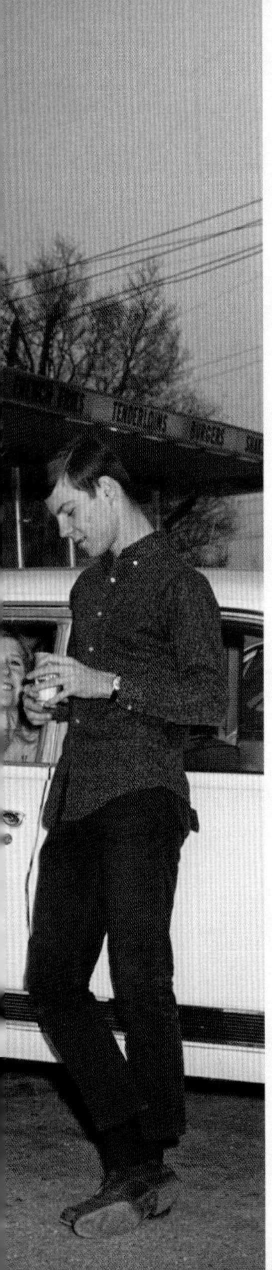

teen scene

Teenagers could get their driver's licenses at age fourteen. In Andrews kids had access to the family sedans and began dragging on Main with radios blaring out the tunes of Elvis, Johnny Mathis, Chuck Berry, Ray Price, Buddy Holly and Roy Orbison and the Teen Kings. When they could beg dad for the keys to the family car, they rounded the course from the newly built Dairy Mart (later known as Scotties) to Jeffery's Steak House. On the way, if they had money, they would stop off at Otto's Ice Cream and listen to the same tunes by putting nickels into the jukebox while eating those wonderful homemade hamburgers and ice cream.

Reba and J.B. Criner

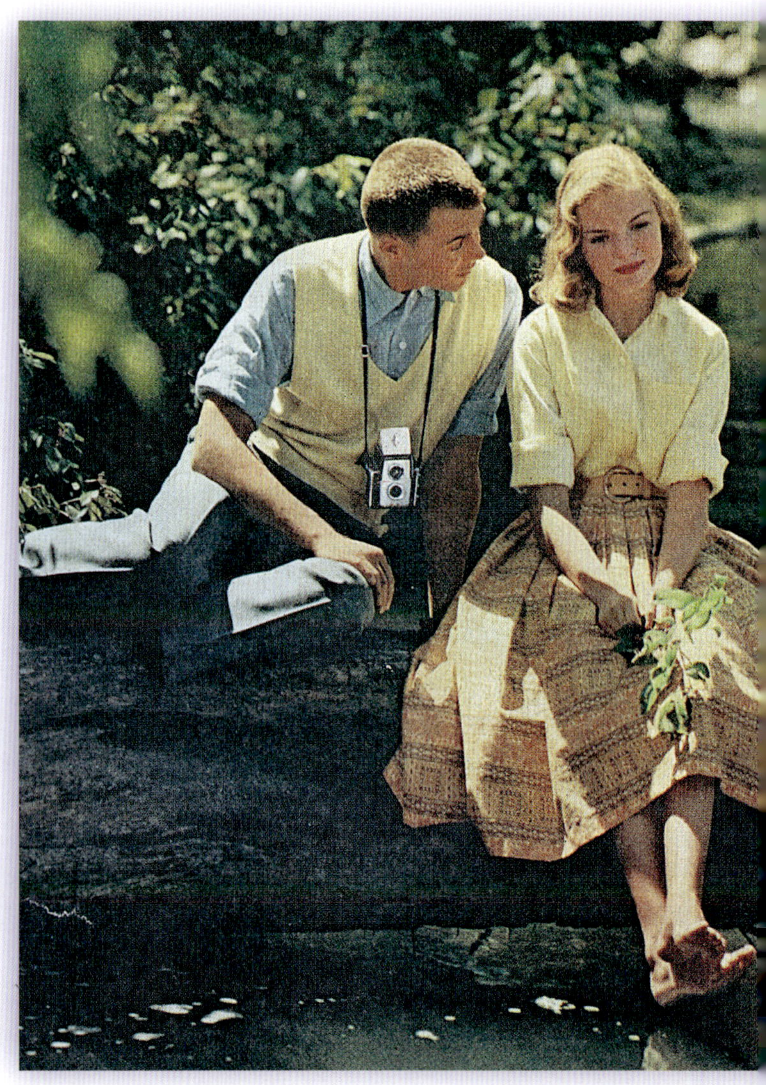

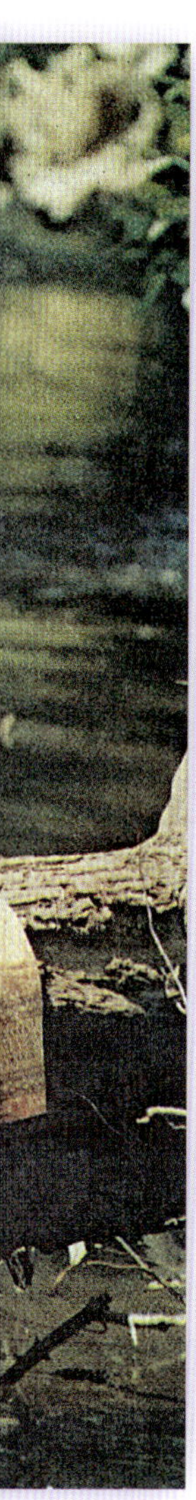

sweet n' shy

I like shy girls. So do other boys I know. We like shy girls and love a real wholehearted blush. Some people mistake shyness for coldness, but they're not the same thing at all. A shy girl answers you, a cold one has no answers. I have four real close friends and a lot of the time we would just sit around and yak about girls. I don't know whether girls yak about boys but I sure know what boys yak about. I don't think there's any question about it: If a girl uses a lot of makeup and talks pretty sophisticated—or swears—you figure either that she's putting on a big front for someone (not me, certainly) or she's fast—or both. And the guys I know aren't interested in dating fast girls. They just aren't. I'm crazy about ponytails, blond ponytails. I don't see anything wrong with parking out in front of a girl's house long enough to say goodnight properly; but heavy necking can only lead to complications we're not ready to handle.

Brandon De Wilde
Photoplay, 1959

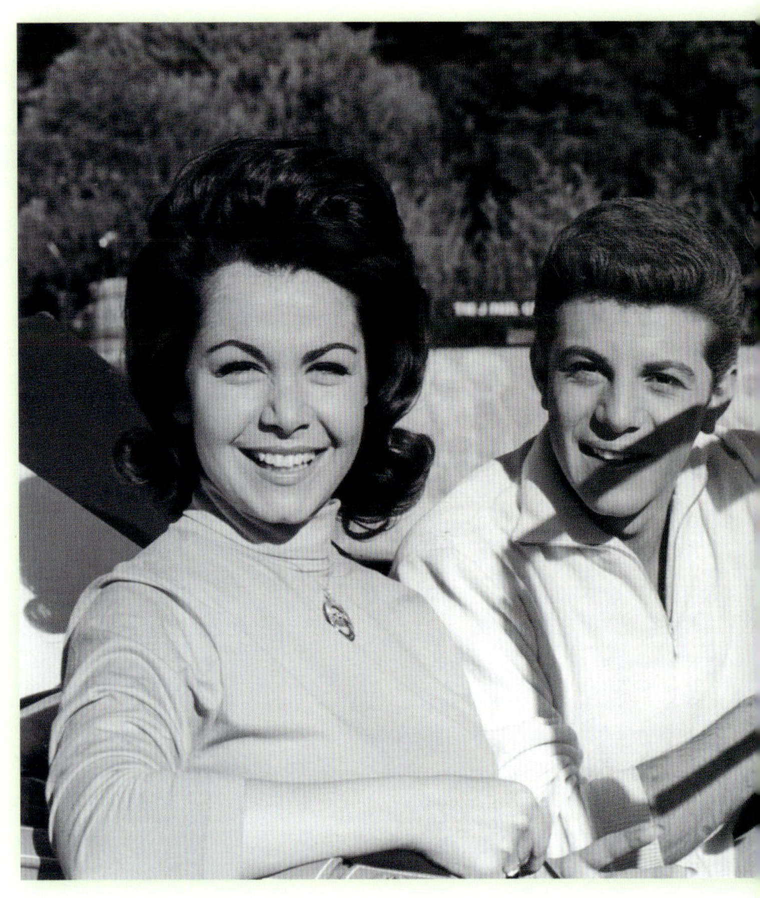

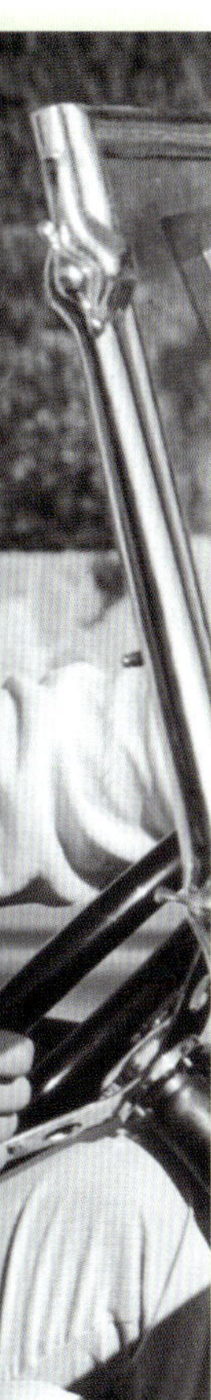

what dads don't know

Cars meant the world back then. They represented freedom from parents and curfews and boredom and the staid 1950s. Boyfriends greased their hair and hid their Lucky Strikes under rolled-up T-shirt sleeves. Elvis: "A Big Hunk o' Love." Chuck Berry: "Oh Baby Doll." Long live rock and roll radio. She wore pleated skirts and saddle oxfords, and kissed boys in the back seat after the sock hops.

"Don't let me catch you going to a drive-in," her dad thundered. What dads don't know can't hurt them.

Jeff Klinkenberg, St. Petersburg Times

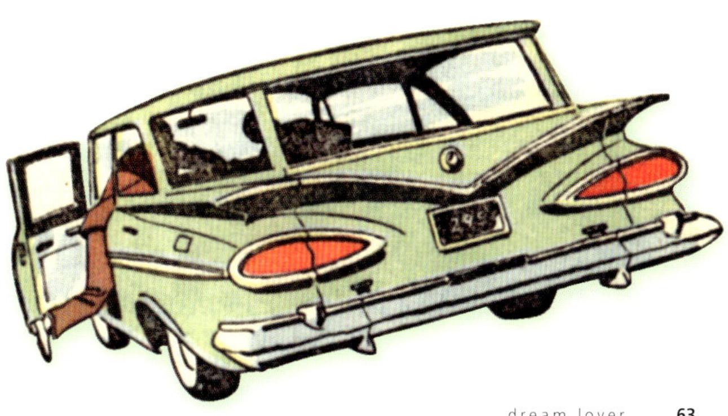

hot date

Drive-ins were the best place for dates. You'd get there, get the cokes and popcorn from the concession stand, and settle down to watch the movie. But that wasn't really the point. The point was about getting as far as you could. I practiced removing a bra with one hand. Remember those bras? They were like armor! The bands were about three-inches wide and stiff, and there were about six hooks and eyes on them. But if you put the heel of your hand on one side of the hooks and you fingers on the other, you could give a sharp squeeze and get all the hooks undone at once. Of course, that's about as far as you got. Any further than that and you'd get a slap. That's what I remember about the '50s.

Jeff Dillon

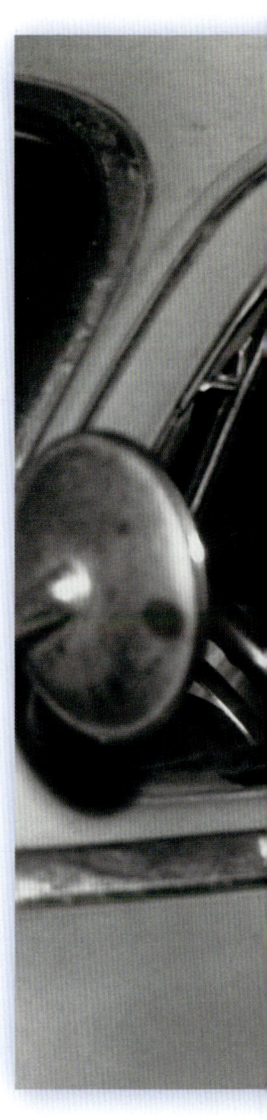

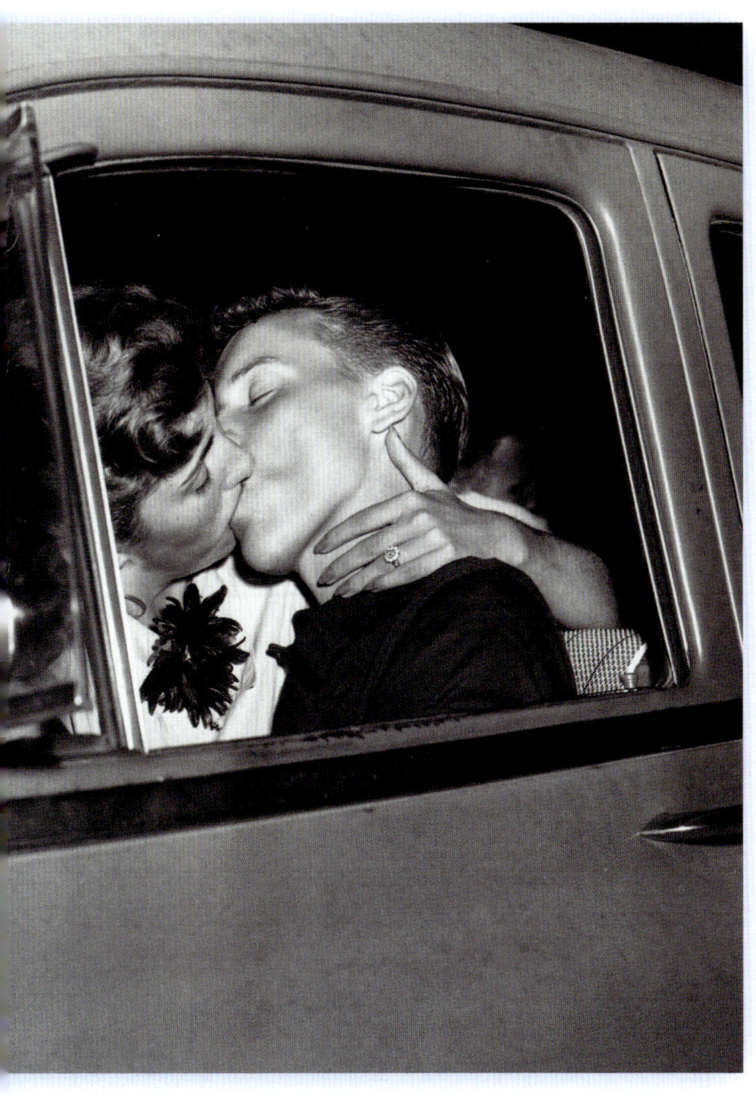

speed dating

Skating rinks were the place to go. Yeah, they were a little rough, but that's how you separated the girls you wanted to date from the ones you didn't. Hey, if she couldn't hold her own at the skating rink—where people going about 20 or 30 miles an hour slammed into her and threw her to the floor—who needed her? I didn't like the ones that cried easy, so I made the skating rink my testing ground.

Jess Parker

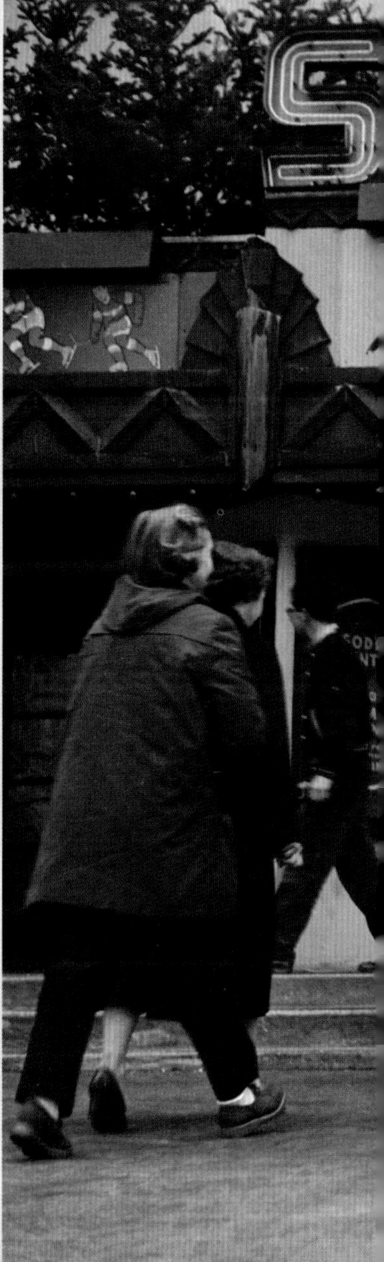

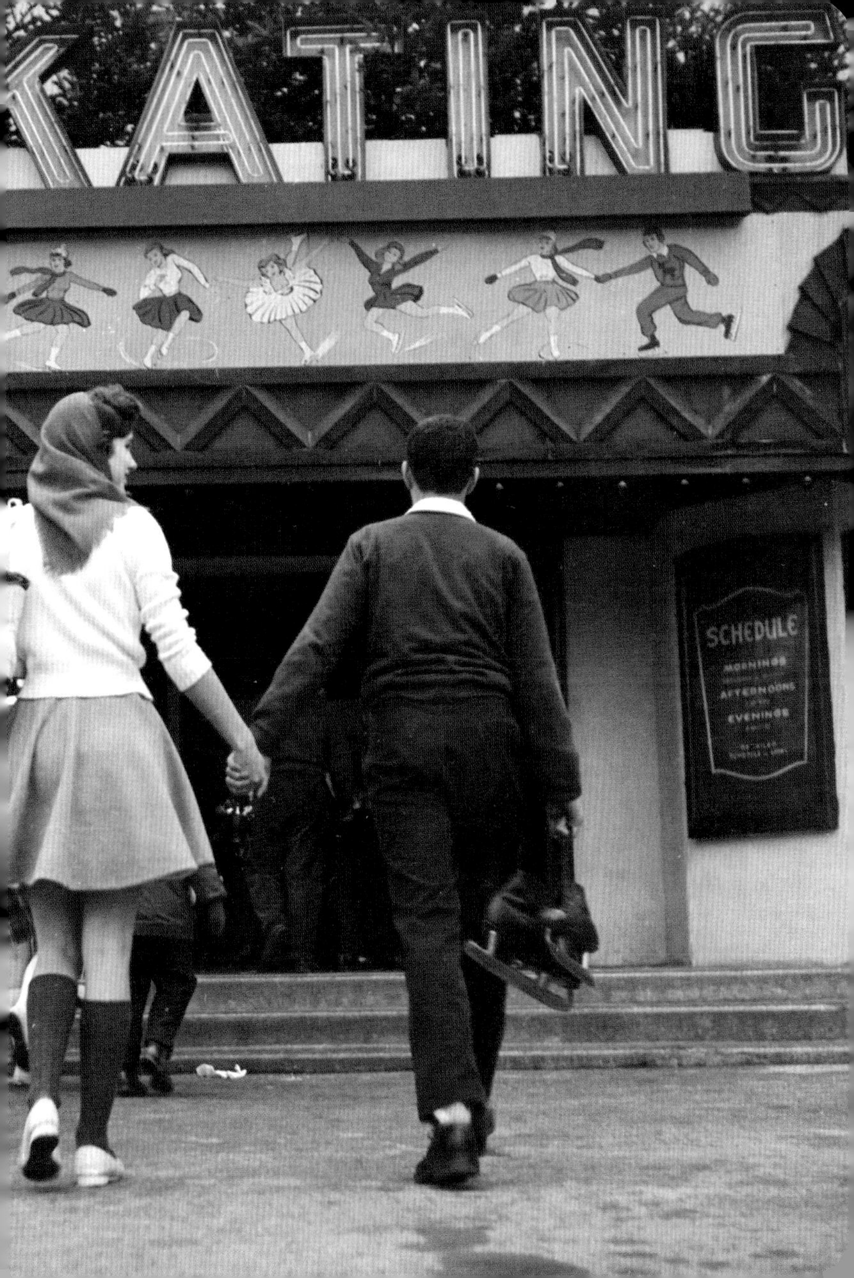
KATING
SCHEDULE
MORNINGS
AFTERNOONS
EVENINGS

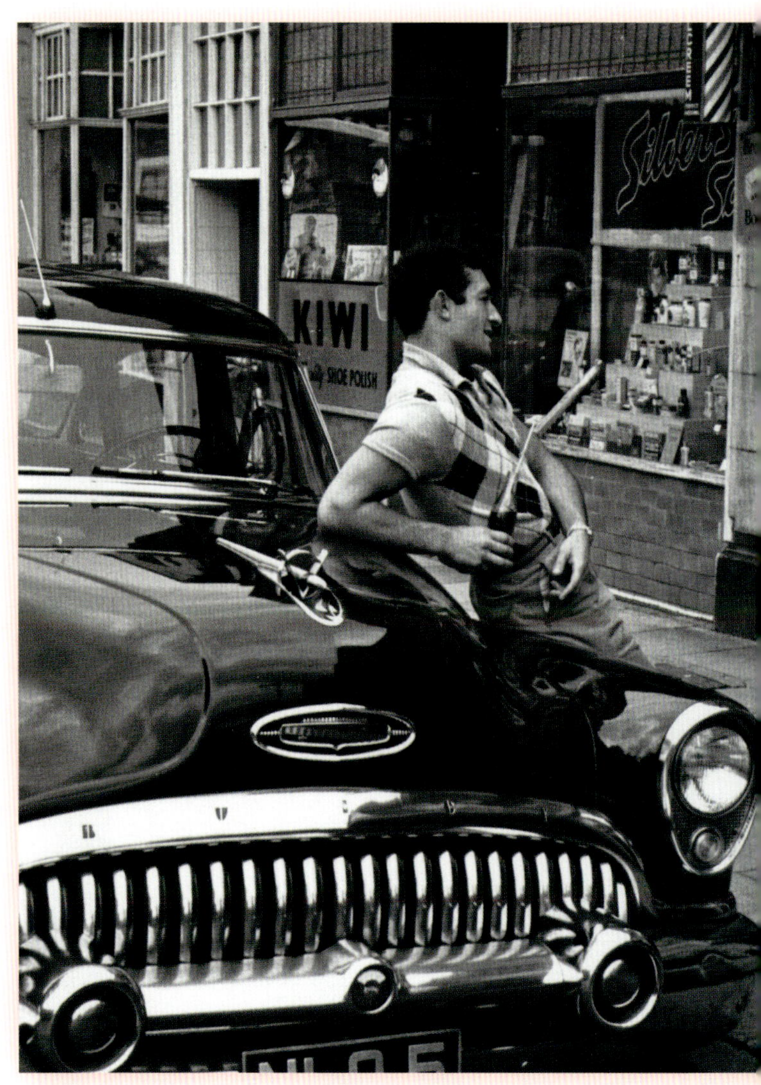
KIWI
SHOE POLISH

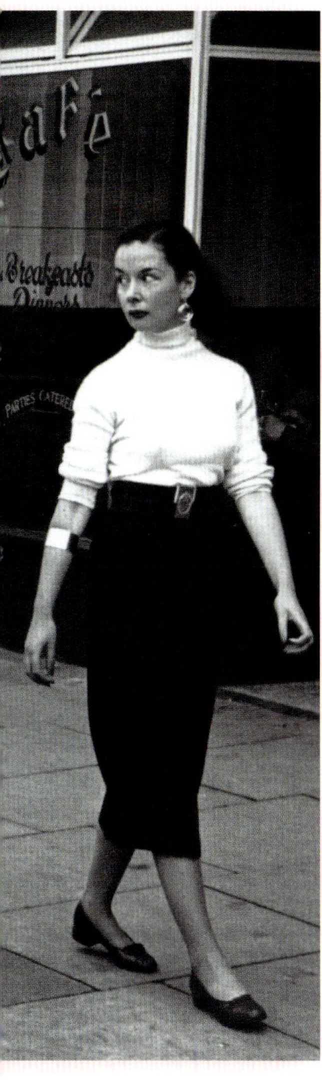

so much yearning!

For a girl, it might have been romance, but for us, it was all about yearning. Listen to the songs, you'll see. We were all obsessed with that which was unavailable at the time—sex. We were in a constant state of desire. That's what the 50s were about if you were young and male. One person in every group always had the stories. It didn't matter if they were true or not; I don't think we even cared. Maybe he was just the guy with the best imagination, the most bravado, and the least inhibitions. We looked forward to every Monday, when we'd listen to him at lunch time or recess. We always hoped he had a good story this week.

Ted Morrison

feeling awkward

Young dating certainly has its hazards, and I guess the main ones are that too often, kids are miserable because they have no social poise, no conversation and feel awkward; they think they'll always feel that way. Then, if they get along with each other and think they're in love, they sort of clutch at each other and go too far. I don't believe, for example, in parking and it's never come up. If it did, I'd say, very soon, "Let's go home," but I've never had to say it. A girl establishes, by her conversation and conduct, what she is and how she wants to be treated, I think. I keep reading and hearing about kids' problems with necking. There are goodnight kisses and there are goodnight kisses! I've said "no" and the boy has asked for other dates—he didn't get angry. A goodnight kiss can be that or it can be the prelude, I should think, to a lot more.

Carol Lynley, Pat Boone Magazine, 1960

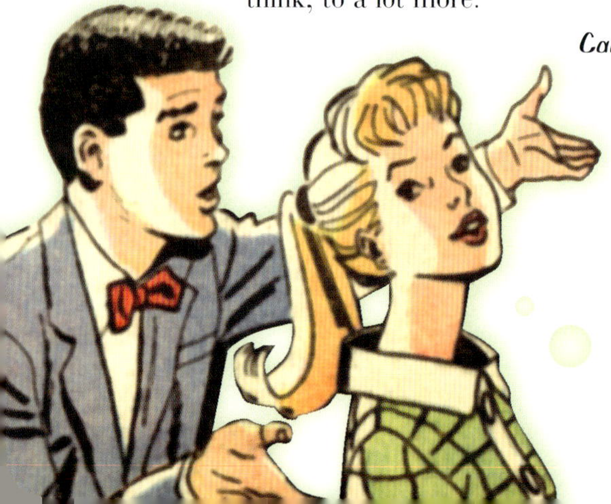

"Let's go home."

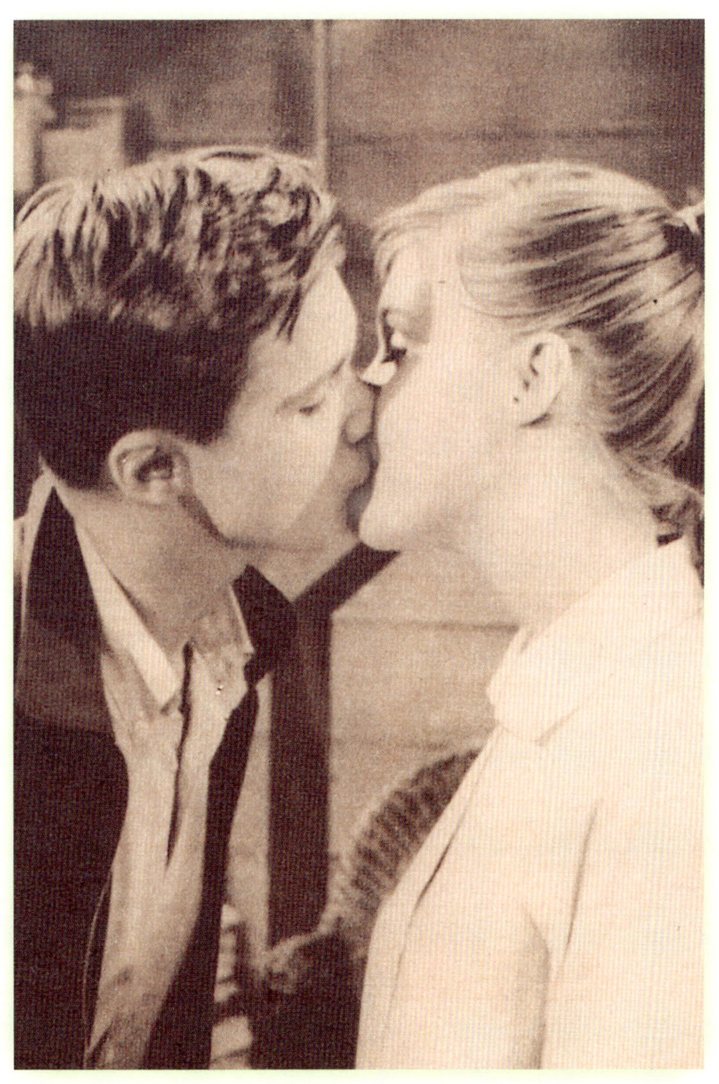

help! I'm in love

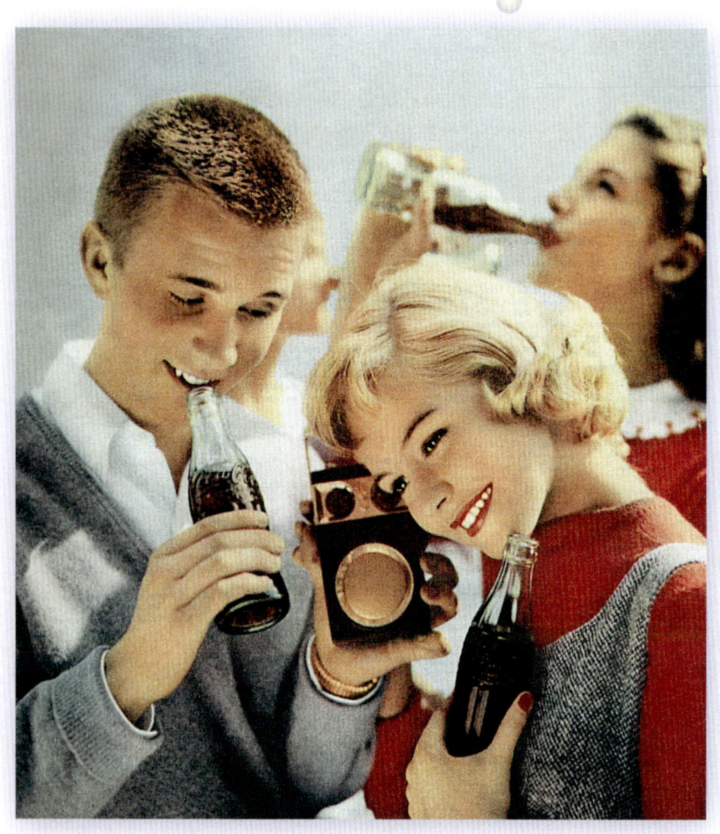

Dear Editor,

I've been dating this one boy pretty steadily since last summer, and my girlfriend Gladys says I should give him a present for his birthday. We haven't known each other very long when I had my birthday so he didn't give me anything. I'd like him to know I appreciate his taking me out, but I don't want to look too pushy.

Sally, Portland, Oregon

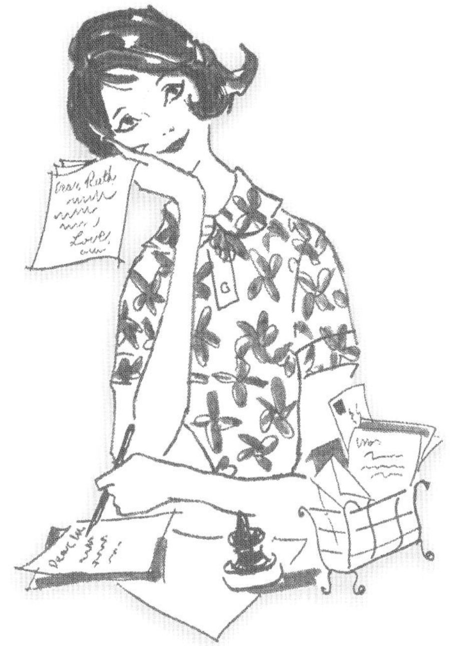

Dear Sally,

A gift could scare a boy away, so think twice before giving one. However, if you've dated for six months, it's quite all right for you to give him a birthday or Christmas present. And you're safest if the gift is inexpensive. We think a book is fun.

Photoplay, 1959

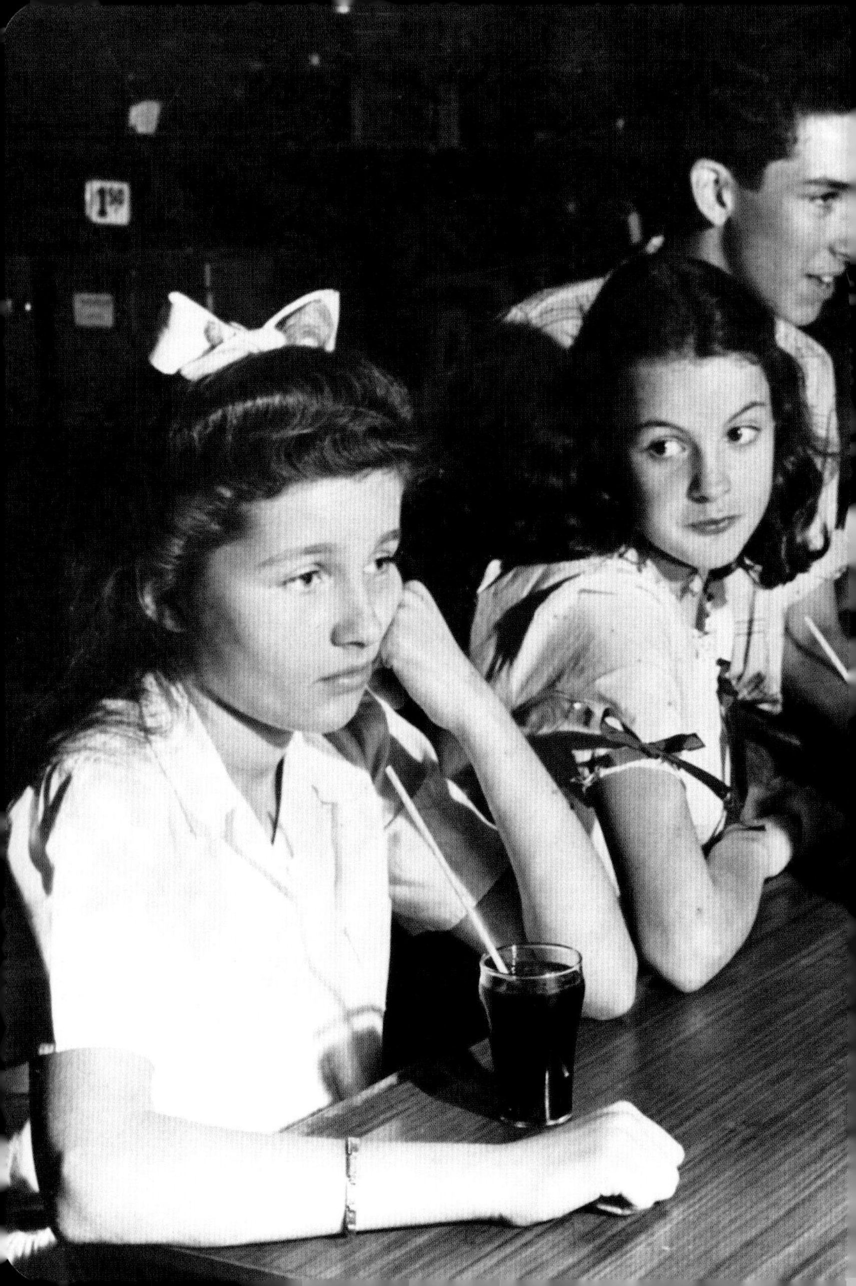

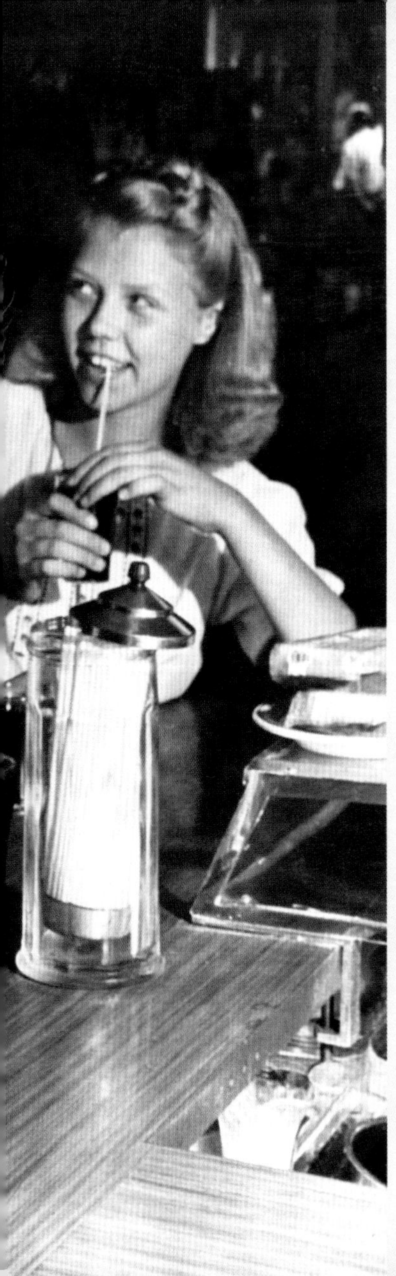

"I'll think of some way to get him back. After all, tomorrow is another day."

Margaret Mitchell
"Gone with the Wind"

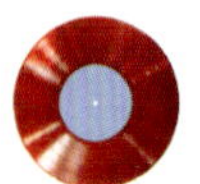

Runaround Sue's Hot Tips for cool dates!

Hi girls. I guess it's time we talk about the most important thing of all—boys! How to snag them, how to keep them, and how to hold them without, well, you know…

Cool Moves: So, you know a really hip guy, but he acts like he doesn't know you're alive. You can't even get him to cast an eyeball in your direction. Well, now! I have a few remedies for that, some cool tricks to make him sit up and take notice.

The first thing you have to do is be where he is. I mean, really, how can he see you unless you're there to be noticed? Pay attention to his habits. Does he go to the drugstore after school or is he watching practice? Wherever he is, you make it a plan to be there, too. Look good, of course, but casual. Give him a nod and a smile, but nothing more at first. You know how it is—guys really don't like the girls that chase them.

But after a couple of weeks of this, of just running into him by accident, you could forget your watch one day. Ask him if he's got the time. You know how to ask. Then carry on the conversation. Ask him another question, something that lets him know you understand that he knows more about the subject than you do.

Friends Can Help: Enlist some aid! Get friendly with

his best friend's girl and fill her in on the scoop. Ask her if she'd be willing to get her fellow to set up a double date. You'd be surprised how well this works.

yakkety yak!

Above the Neck: Some guys just can't be trusted. You think everything is cool, that he understands that when you say you're fine with necking, but no petting, please! So if he strays, if his hands start moving toward a place they shouldn't be, you have no choice but to remind him of your rule: keep it above the neck if you want to stay on the deck.

Influence his Decision: Tie a mirror warmer to his rear view vision, and smile at him when you do. Tell him it's to remember you when you're not there. See what he says. If he leaves it there, you're one step closer to that ring.

TV Dates: You know, girls, getting out and around can get expensive for a guy. And if your fellow's really worth it, he'll never let you pay. But maybe he just can't raise the bread. So give it a thought. What would you prefer? To stay home alone on Friday night, or ask him to be there? Ask him over for a TV date. Clear it with the folks, of course, and then lay in some snacks. You'll be surprised how nice this is, to have him in your home.

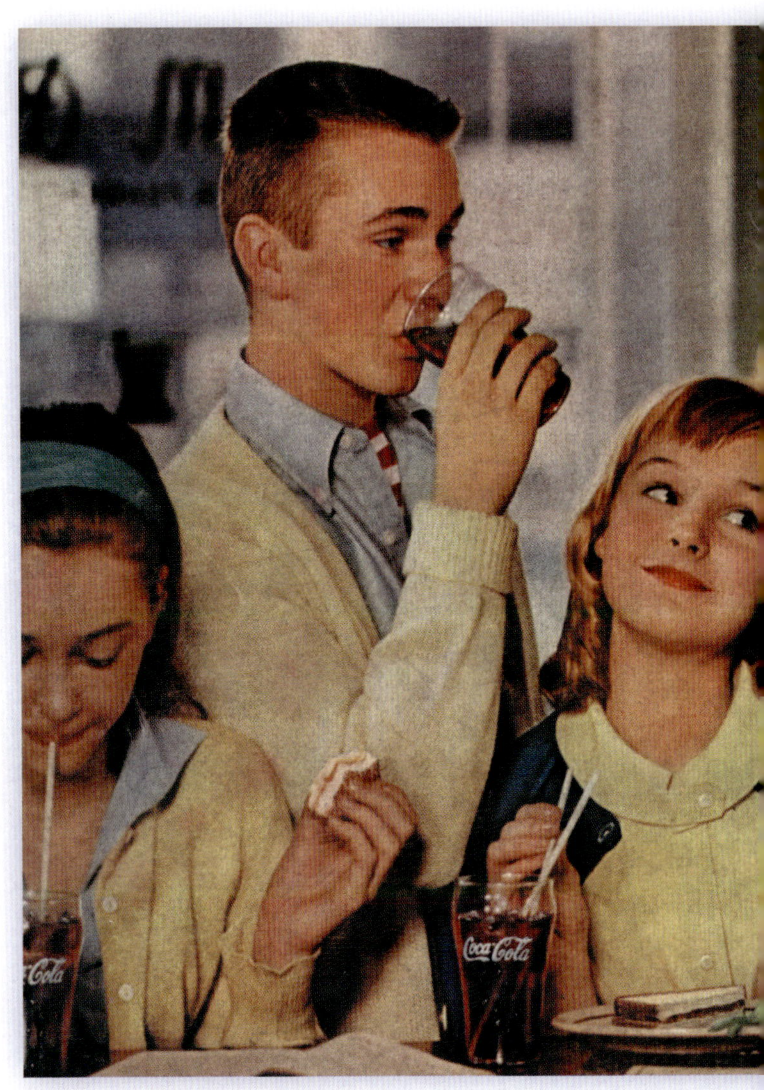
Coca-Cola

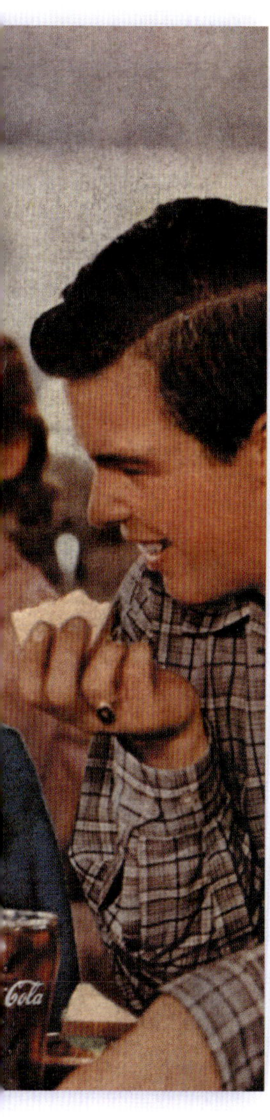

so secure

Some boys want a girl who is full of adventure—who is a different person each time they're together…but I don't. I want to be loved and to feel secure with my girl.

Bobby Vee

"I just want to be loved."

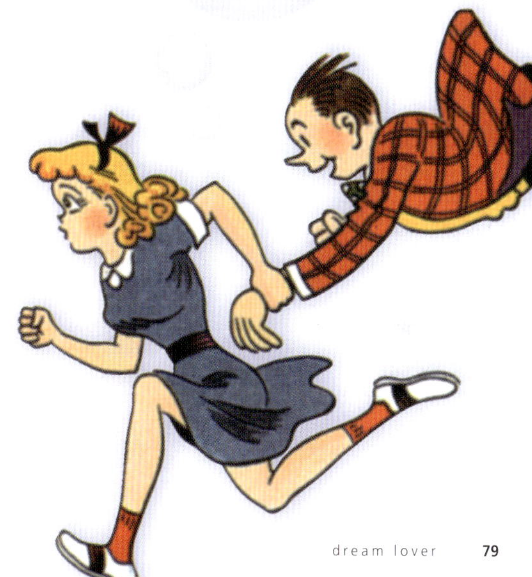

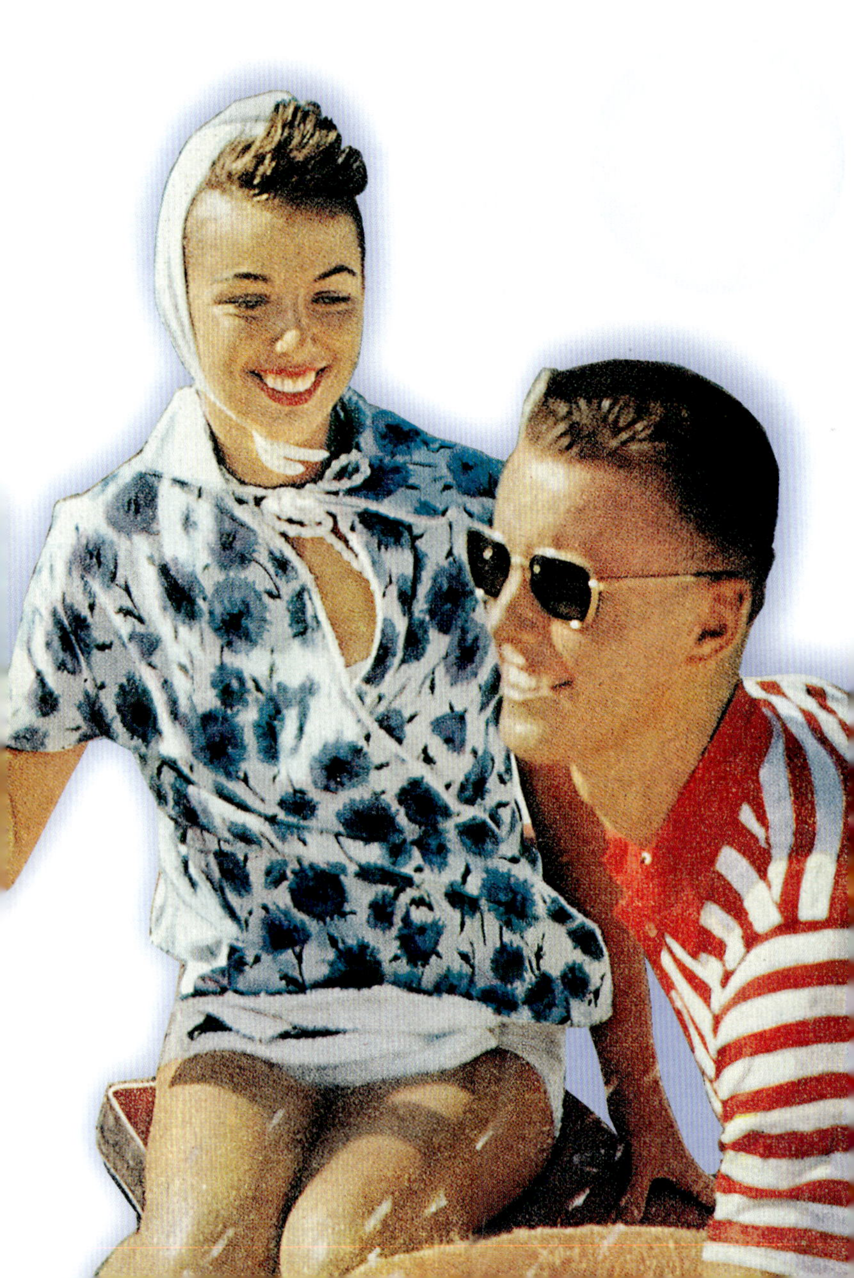

Chapter 4

BLUE SUEDE SHOES

Style? The hip young things of the 1950s had it buttoned down real tight! They were sassy and slick, cute and cool—from top to toe. Hair had to be just right: ponytails for girls, flattops or pompadours for guys, and Elvis sideburns—and they spent hours fixing it all in the mirror! They all wore pegged jeans, though girls also adored feminine skirts with saddle shoes and bobby socks. Demure, maybe, but devastatingly pretty.

I saved up till I finally had enough for a poodle skirt—the one you could buy at The Young Colony Shop. Nice, thick felt—mine was that flecked grey color—with a red leash for the poodle, and a nice rhinestone in his eye. It fell just right, thick folds at the bottom, nothing flimsy about it.

Patti Smith

slick'n'stylish

Did you think guys were not supposed to care about their hair? Well, let me tell you something! We were as vain as that guy Kookie in the TV program 77 Sunset Strip—and he was always combing his hair! When the DA came onto the scene, we elbowed our sisters for time at the bathroom mirror, and spent hours in the men's room combing our hair. Oh, yeah, and I had a special metal comb that I kept in the back pocket of my jeans. To tell the truth, I could fix my hair blindfold if necessary!

Bruce Walker

"Kookie, Kookie, lend me your comb!"

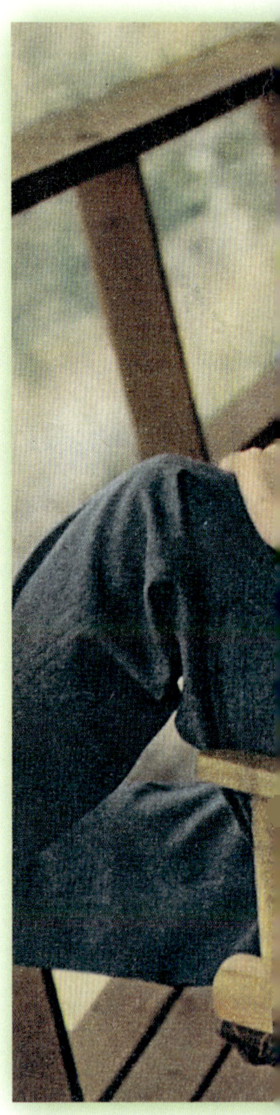

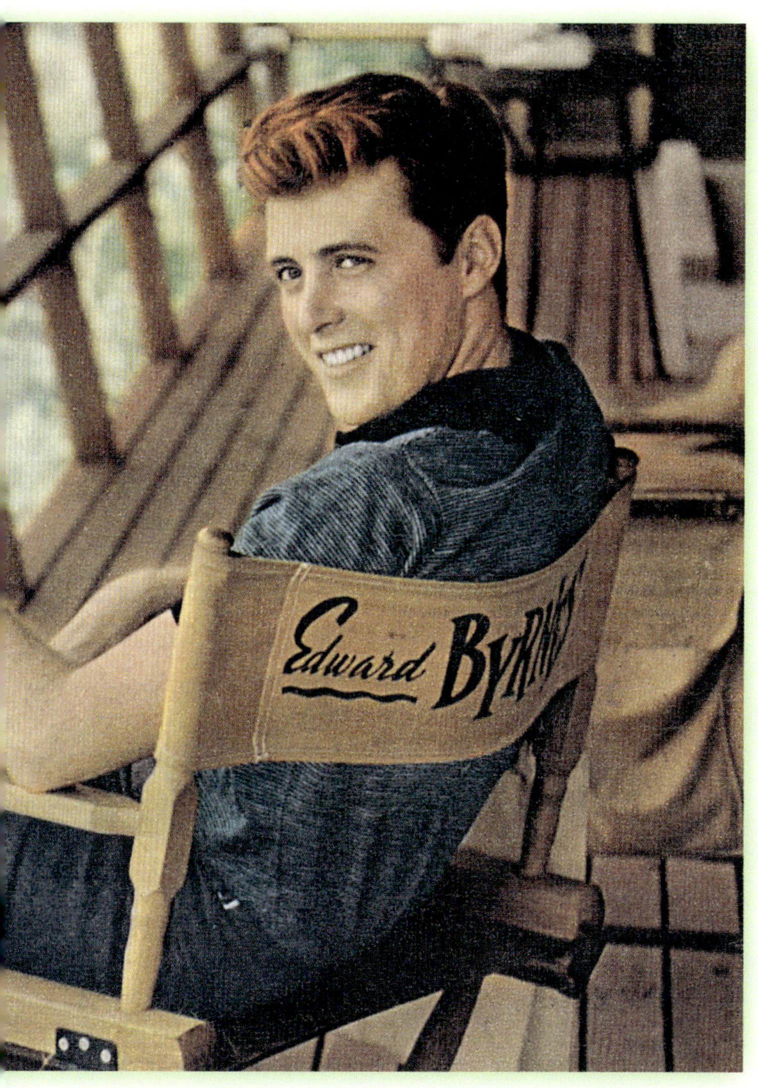
Edward

all that hair stuff!

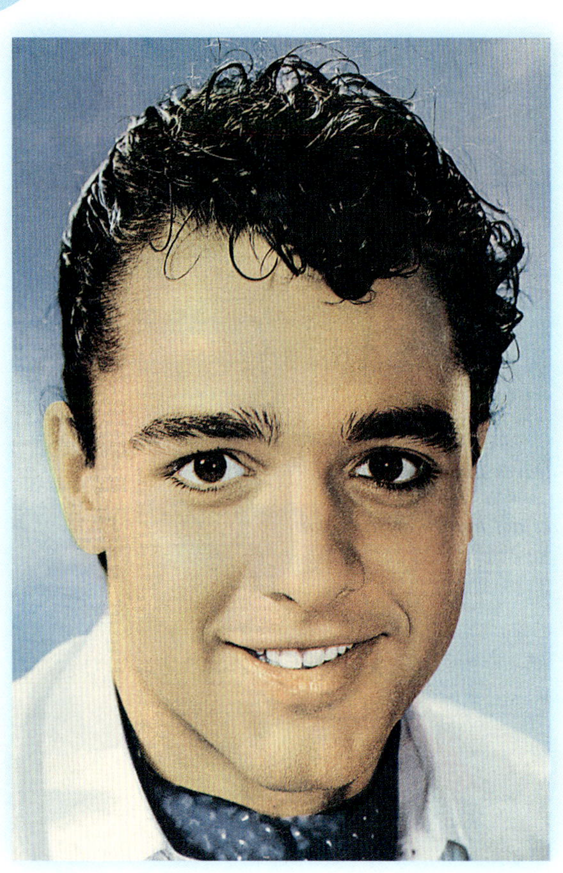

My first flattop was a big deal for me, I guess, because I was the first person in my school to have one. And it was so new that the local barber didn't even have that metal grate they used to get it even—I had to get into the city to get it cut for a couple of months. The choice of hair stuff was important too. You needed wax. Same if you had a DA—you needed wax. Butch wax—that was the favorite. If you had a pomp or pompadour like Sal Mineo, you had to use some kind of grease to keep it in place: there was Wild Root, which had a strong fragrance, or Troll, which was a bright green color.

Jon Rutherford

"So how much of that butch wax did you use?"

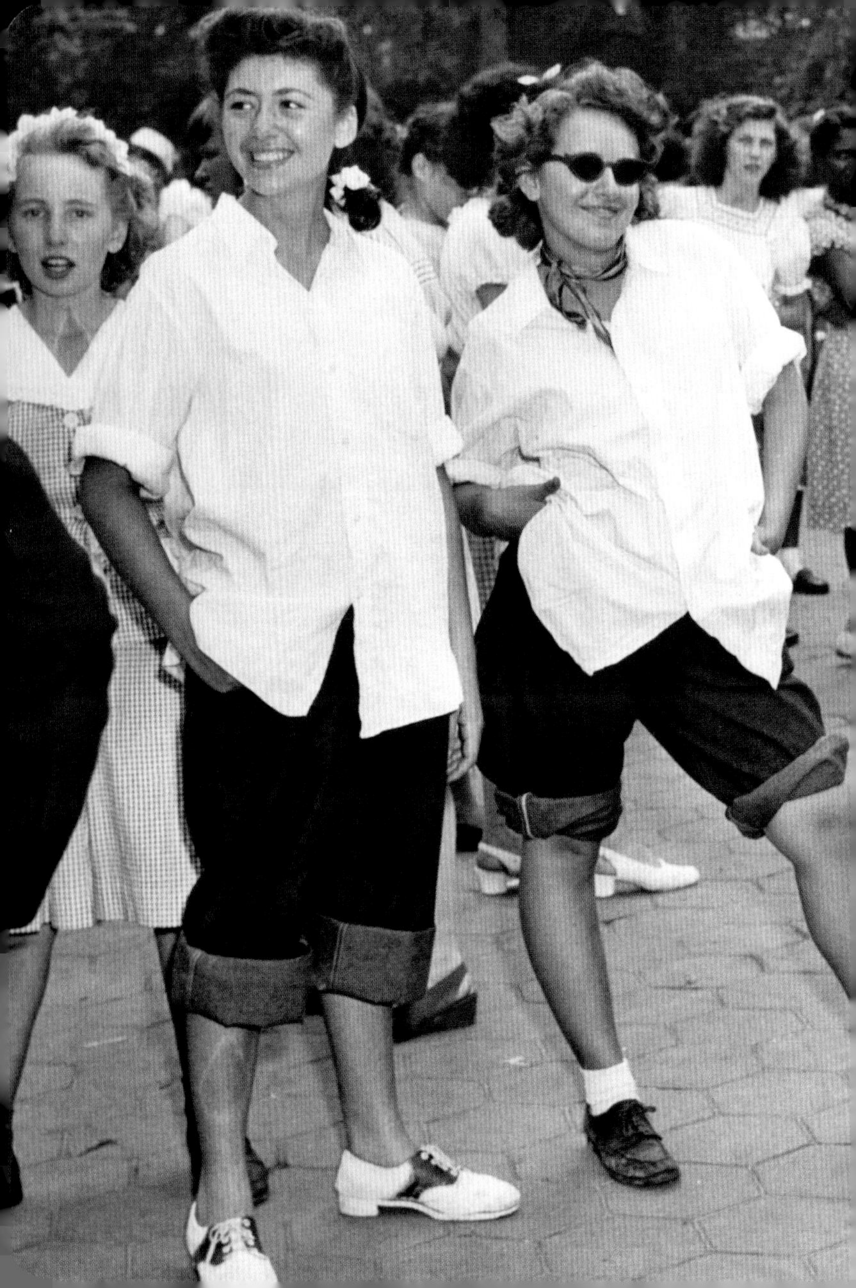

peggin' the pants

I never did get the hang of pegging my pants. You were supposed to make a fold at the bottom of your pants—fold them over to make a flap—and then stick them in your boots like that, so the fold stayed in. It never did on me. Plenty of girls I knew wore their jeans rolled up just under the knee—that was their way to look cool at the time.

Mel Brodecky

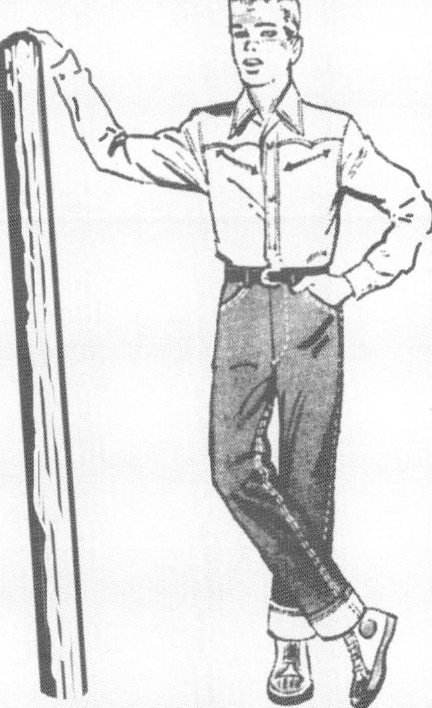

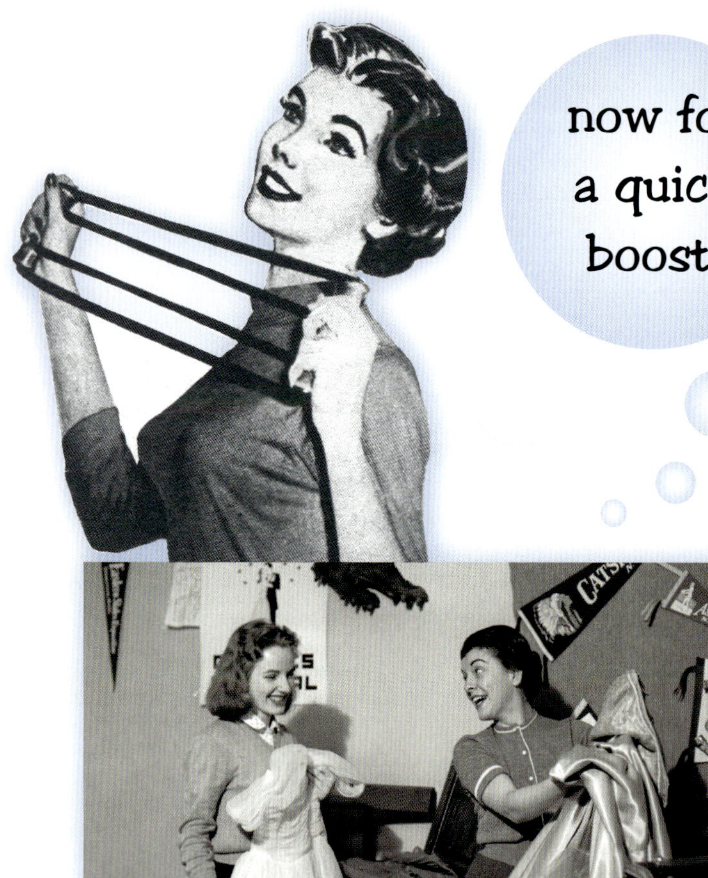

now for
a quick
boost!

I knew people who stuffed their bras with toilet paper. I had the opposite problem, which was bad if the gym teacher made you run or play sports, but was a definite asset in the dating arena. But anyway, I'll tell you this: Those girls who stuffed their bras with wadded-up toilet paper protected their bra hooks—no one ever unhooked their bras without a sharp slap. So I guess mothers everywhere wished we all needed to add some stuffing.

Annie L. George

"If any guy tries anything on me he's going to get a slap!"

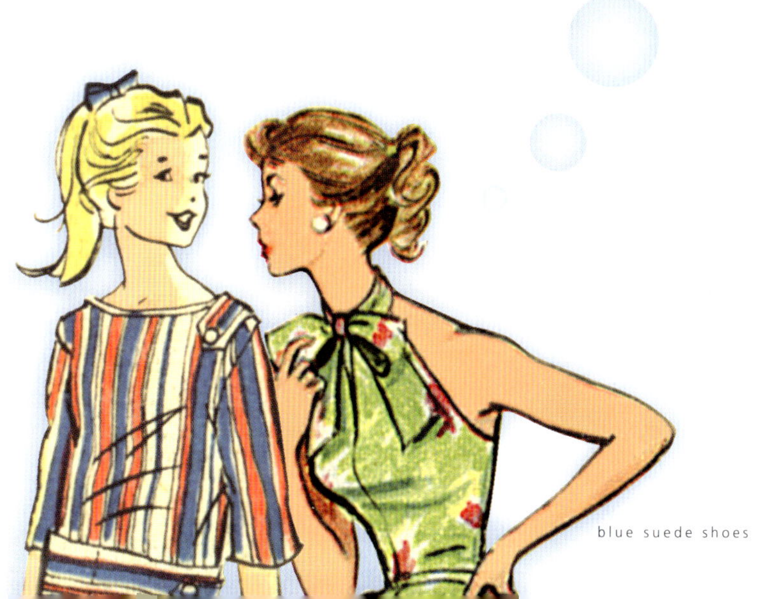

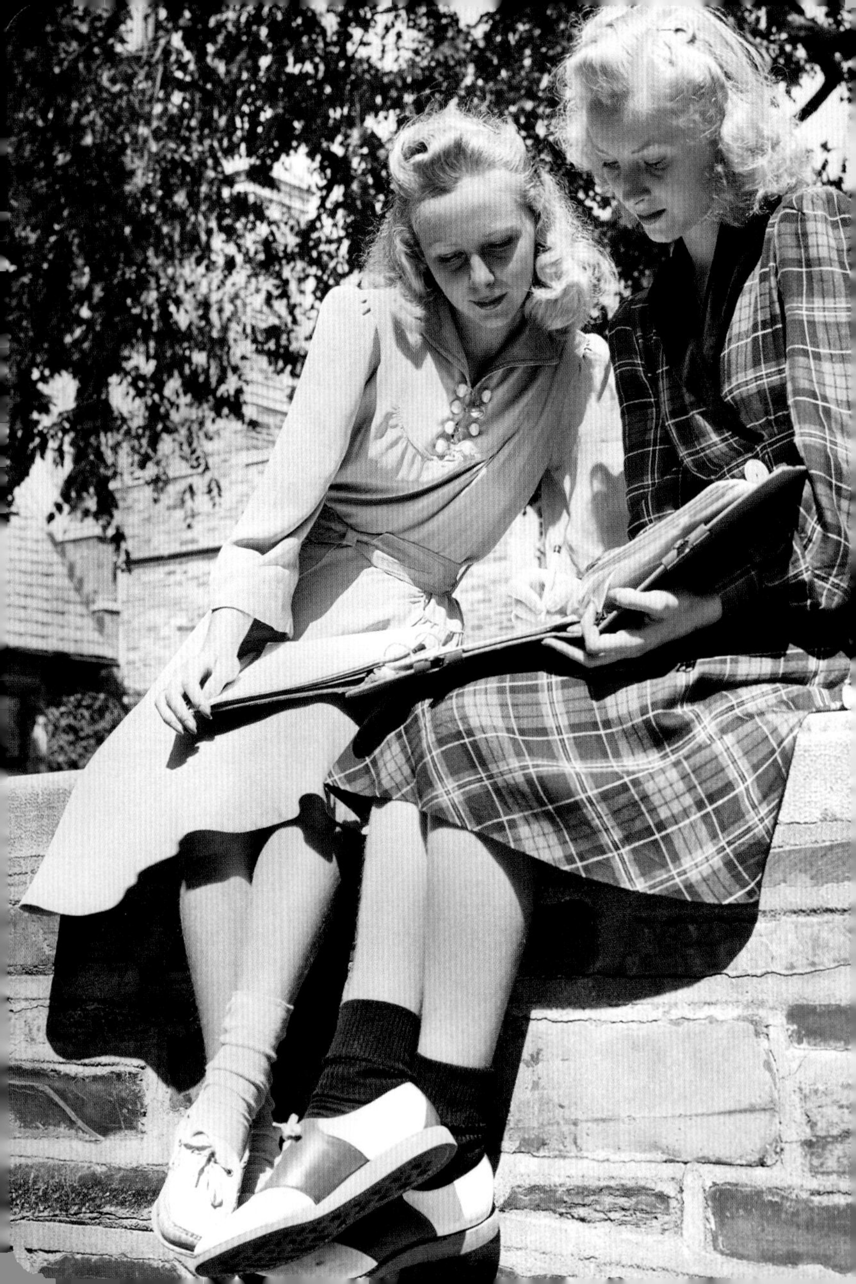

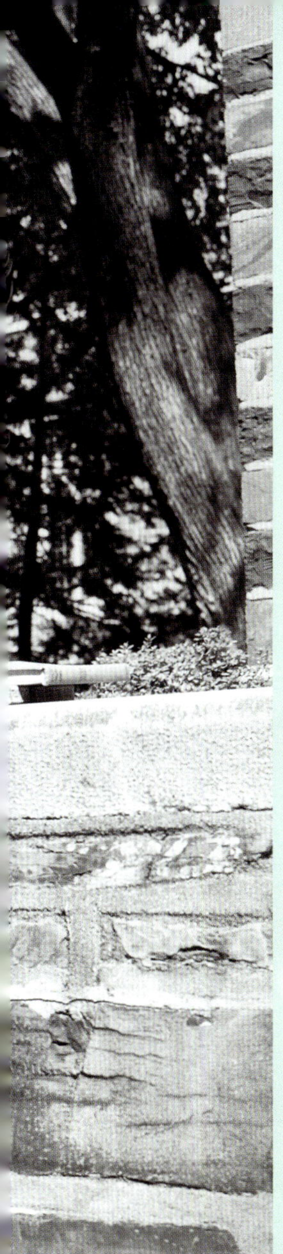

fancy footwork

Keeping my saddle-shoes white was a Sunday night chore. Every Sunday night, Ed Sullivan or no Ed Sullivan, I polished those shoes. I bleached my socks, too. I wasn't allowed to do that—"bleach wears out your clothes too fast," said my mother—but I did it on the sly. I'd wash my socks when she wasn't around, so she never knew.

Mary Lou Shepherd

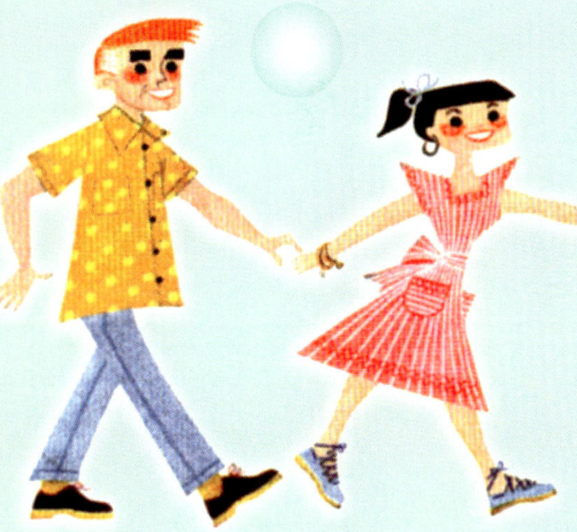

Pink rollers. I slept in them. And setting lotion—gloppy, pink, stinky, sticky setting lotion. That was in the days when you washed your hair only once a week—more was considered both wasteful of water and bad for your hair, so it got really stiff by the end of the week. I learned to wash it Thursday night so it would look good for the weekend—these were also the days when it never looked good the day after you washed it. By Friday night, it looked OK, but never on Friday morning. I think it's a matter of conditioner, but I'm not sure. All I know is that you had to wait a day for it to look really good. That and sleep on rollers. Or rag-ties or pin curls. But once rollers came in, we never went back to bobby pins or rag-ties.

Miranda Smith

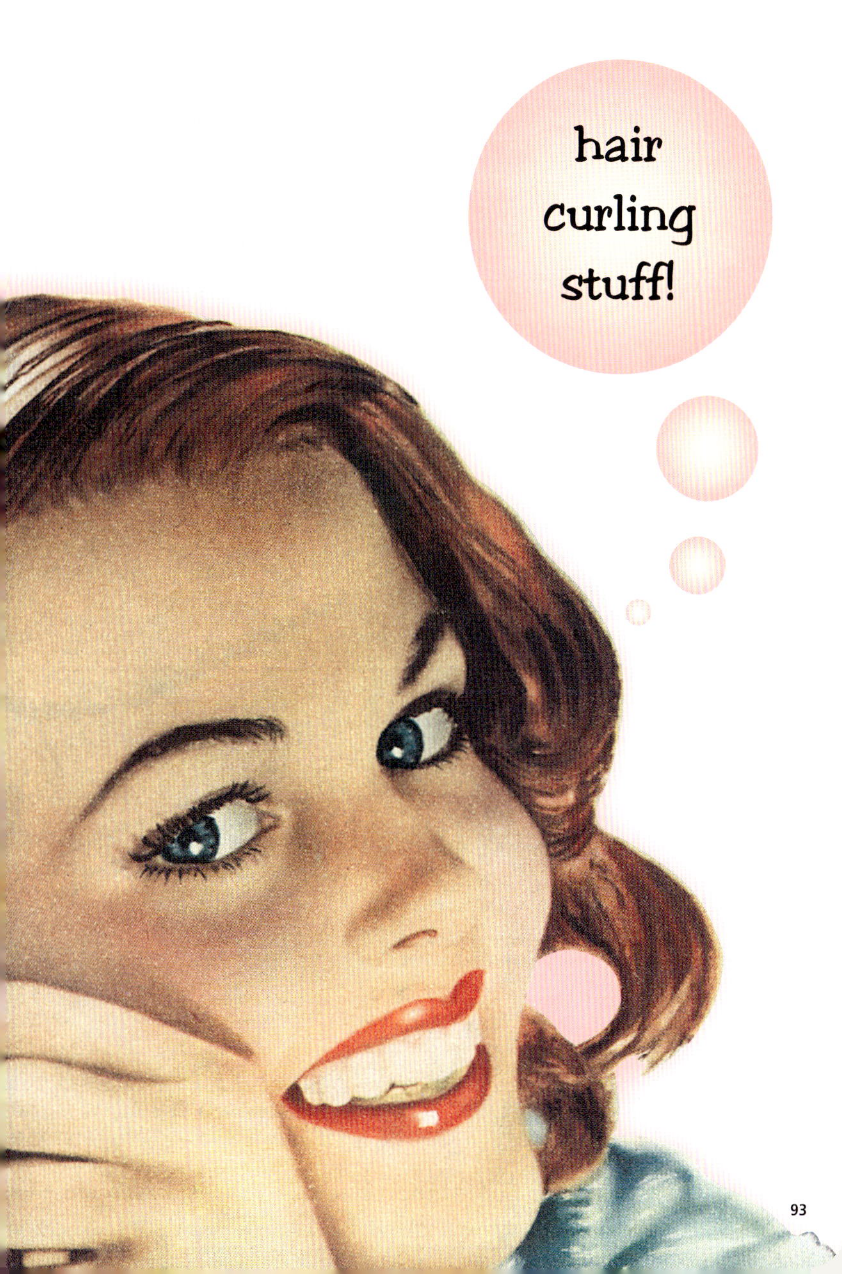
hair
curling
stuff!

Runaround Sue's Hot Tips for the cutest look ever!

Hi. Want to know what's buzzin for your lashes? How to make like Betty Boop with the eyes? Well, here's the scoop. Put on your mascara as usual, no change. But just before it's dry, shake a little face powder over your lashes. Then brush on more mascara—the powder that's stuck to your lashes makes them so thick and long, you'll make the Fuller Brush man turn a sick shade of green.

yakkety yak!

Here's another crazy powder trick, but this one's for the lips. The next time you pull out your favorite stick, take out your compact too. Put that lipstick on, but don't blot. Instead, pat your face powder over your lips. Wait a minute and put on that special shade again—this is so cool. When you tell a guy to get lost and take a powder, he'll split if he's hip. But if you take a powder to your lips, your color's gonna stick.

Hey, girls! Does your old setting lotion flake? By the end of the week, does it look like you have a serious case of dandruff? Well, don't worry! I just learned the coolest way to chase those flakes to splitsville—give them a stocking to run off with! That's right, a stocking. Cover the bristles of your hair brush with an old nylon stocking—one with a run in it—and brush those flakes away.

Keep checking the brush—when the stocking looks like a snow-covered peak, move the brush to a new spot. And if your hair is oily and you just can't get to washing it—use baby powder. Sprinkle it on your hair and let it sit for a few minutes to absorb the oil. Then brush again, still with the stocking over the brush. And remember girls—it takes a hundred strokes a day to keep your crowning glory glorious!

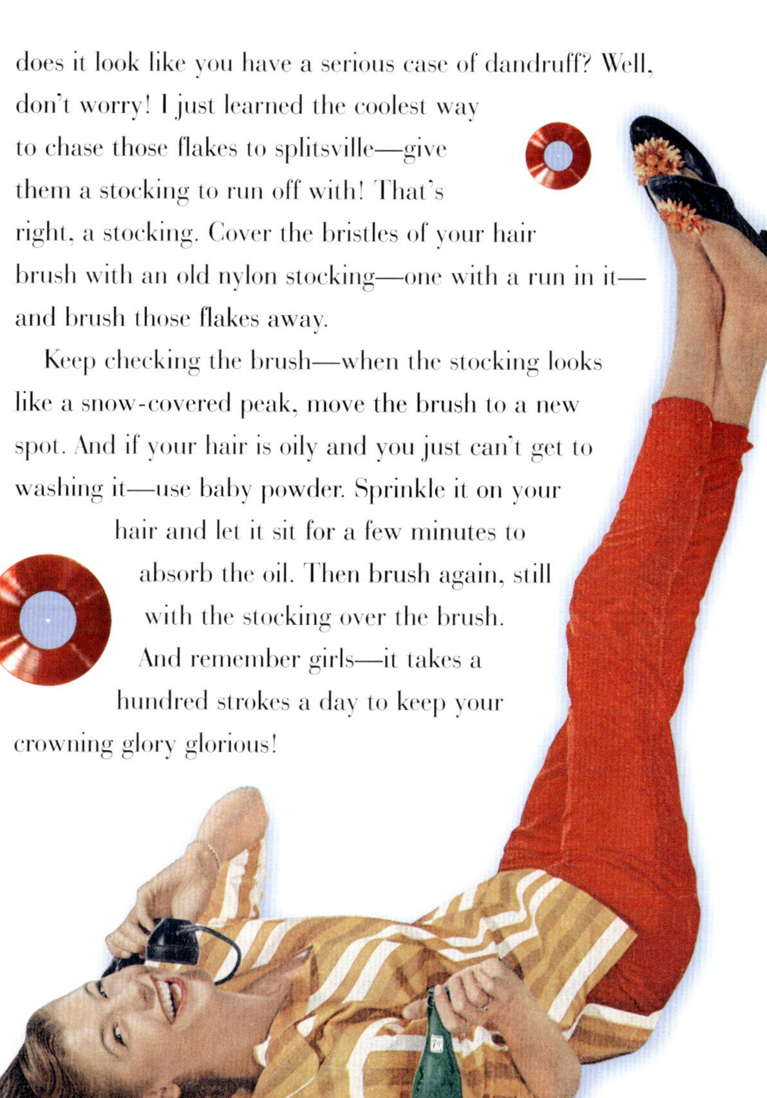

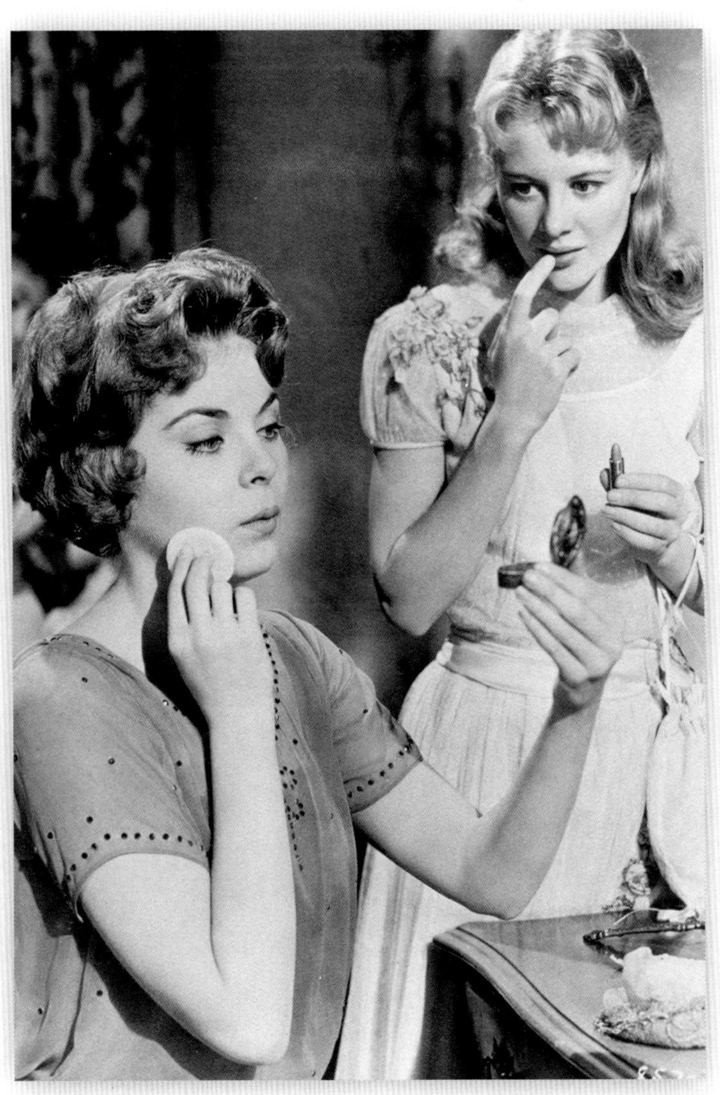

a little makeup!

Most parents didn't allow makeup. But that meant nothing to us. We all kept it in our lockers, along with a jar of cold cream and a box of tissues. In the morning, we'd race into school, long before the first bell, and head for the girls' room. It was so crowded in there that you usually had to stoop to find an empty spot at the mirror. But you did. And you'd apply mascara—Maybelline in the pink case, just as it comes today. And lipstick. No rouge for me—I thought I was too rosy as it was, so I used powder to try to tone it down. But the big thing was eyeliner. My mother might ignore a little lipstick and mascara, but if she'd ever seen that eyeliner, I woulda been grounded, for sure. Fortunately, the cold cream worked—last period, we'd always get excused for the ladies' and take it all off. When we couldn't do that, we'd do it on the bus.

"Just a little touch of rouge, dear."

Ginger Farrell

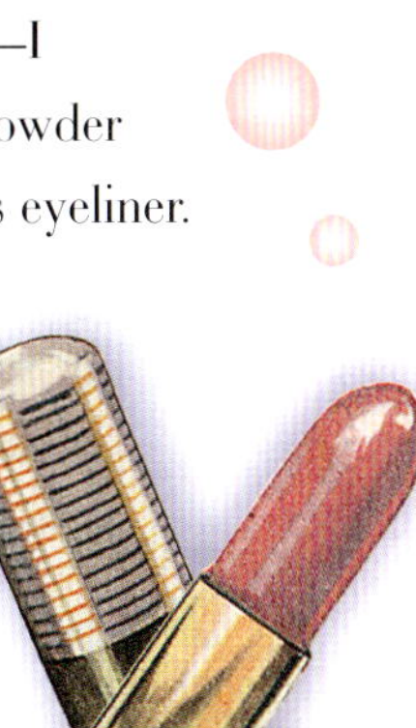

teenie-bopper style

In the lower grades boys wore black Converse tennis shoes and played touch football on the playground while the girls wore ponytails and played jacks, jump rope, and paper dolls. We played "Annie Over" and "Kick the Can" and slept outside in the summer. The girls had slumber parties and the boys tried to crash them. Teenage teenie-boppers wore petticoats made from miles of netting to help those wide skirts stand out over bobby socks and penny loafers or saddle oxfords. The boys wore Levi jeans with a cuff and white socks in buckskin shoes.

Reba and J.B. Criner

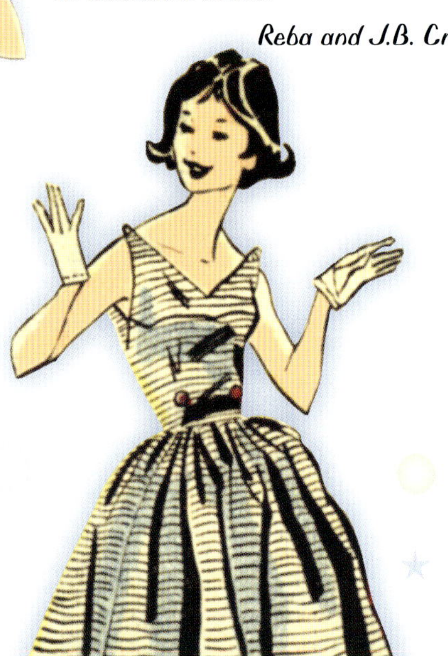

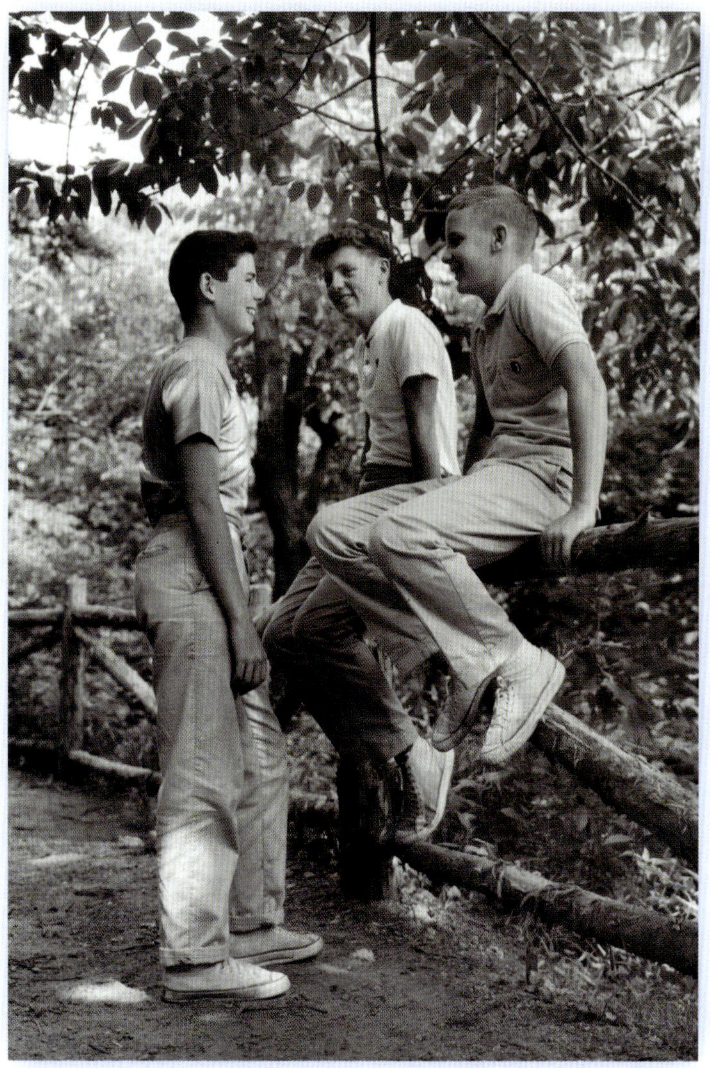

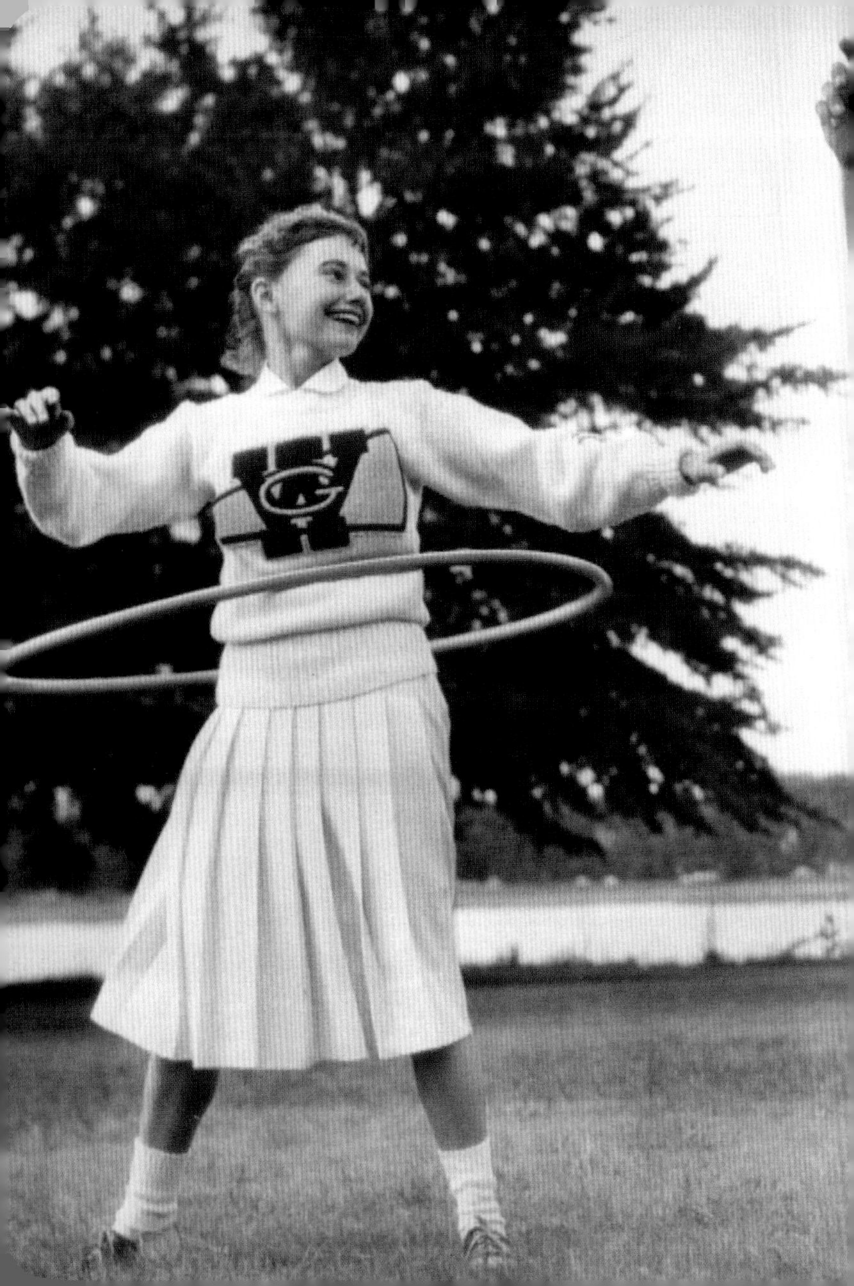

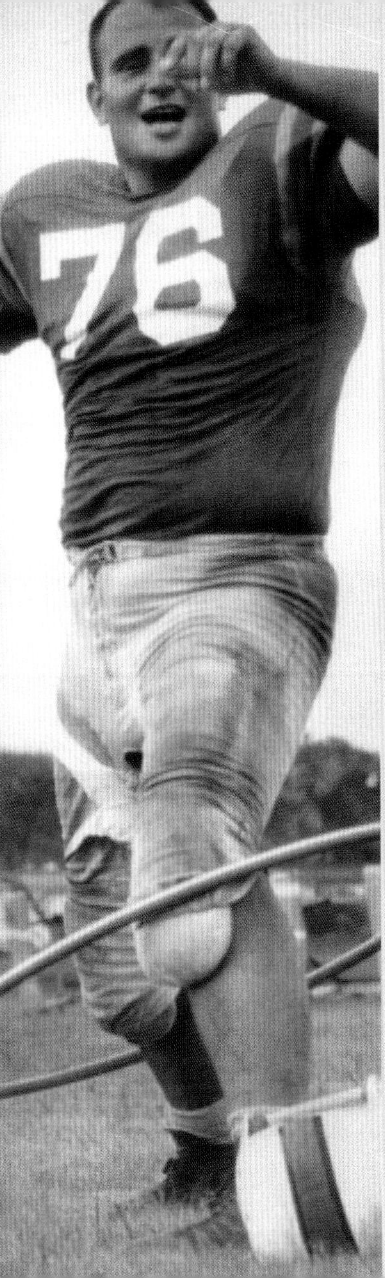

hula hoops

These brightly colored plastic hoops were manufactured by the Wham-O Company, and became the biggest fad of all time! Everyone was spinning a hula hoop—some people managed to keep several going at the same time. There were competitions to see who could keep the hoops spinning longest. Hula hoops were so popular, stores kept running out of supplies—over 20 million were sold in the first six months.

"There you go again, Joe, letting the side down!"

think pink!

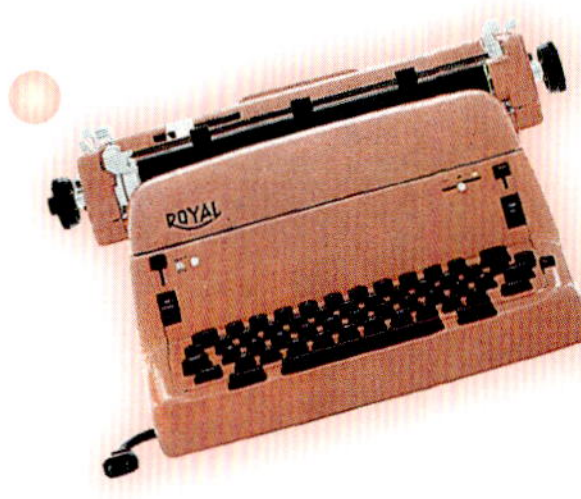

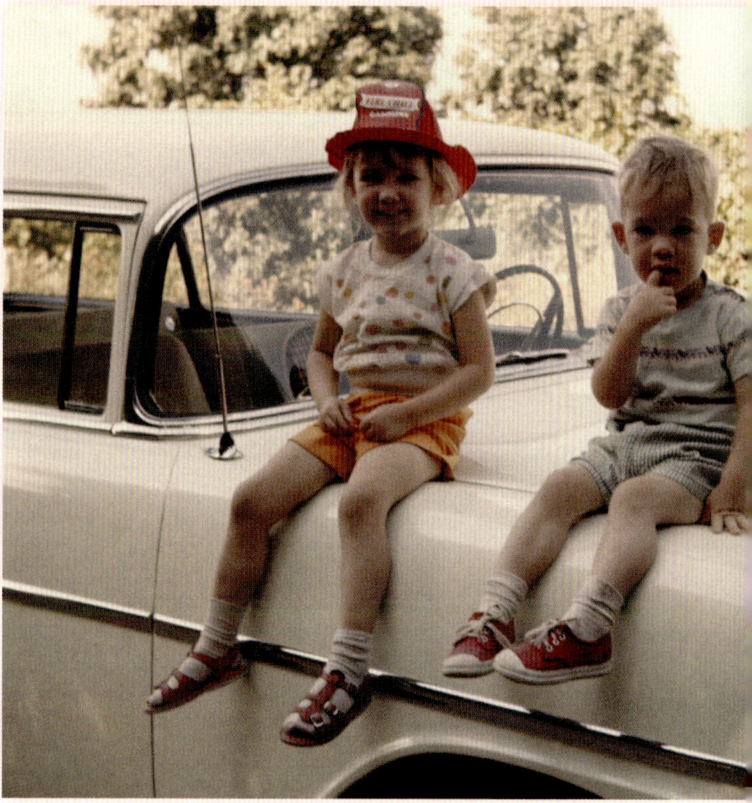

The 1950s brought a rush of color into everyday life—a welcome reaction to the drab years that went before. But the most noticeable was pink. It was everywhere. There were pink cars, pink bathrooms, pink cosmetics and of course, the obligatory pink poodle. Elvis Presley was famous for wearing pink jackets and also owned a collection of pink Cadillacs. Previously, pink was a color strictly for the girls; now it even pervaded menswear. Men commonly wore pink ties, shirts, and bathrobes. Even serious business types wore pink shirts under their dark suits. Like many fashions of the time, it was a temporary fad. But it certainly made its mark.

Sue Trimmer

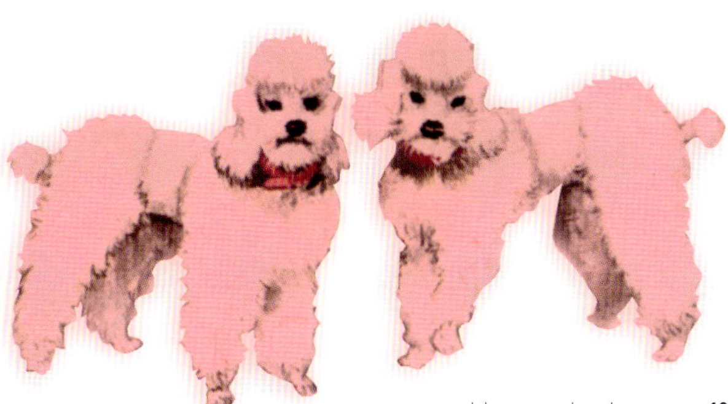

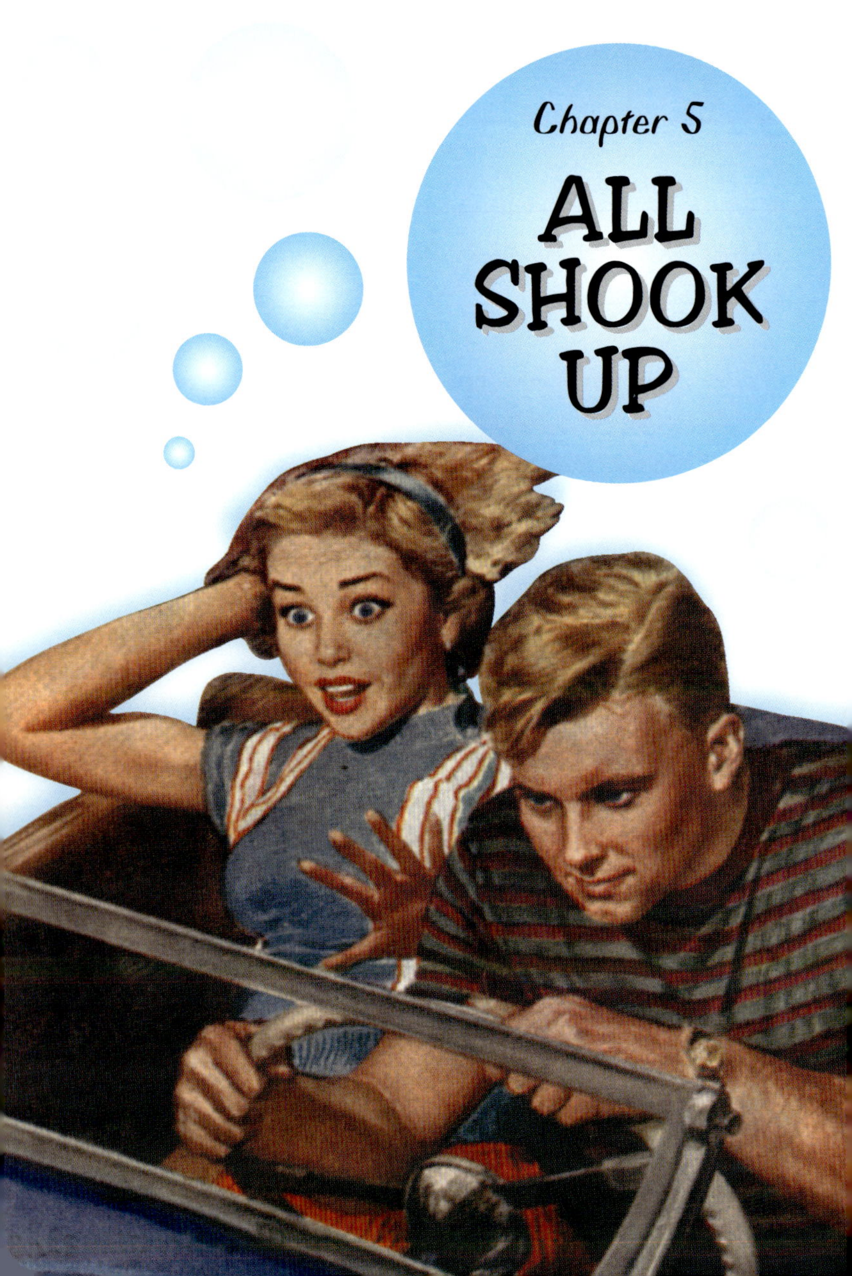
Chapter 5
ALL SHOOK UP

The new-found pleasures of the 1950s brought young people into sharp conflict with the older generation—particularly on the subject of rock and roll! Many parents hated it; some church leaders condemned it—but teenagers adored it! Rock and roll had a huge impact on youth culture, affecting everything from the clothes young people wore, to how they danced. When the movie "Rock Around the Clock" was released, excited fans got up and jived in the aisles of the movie theaters. Older, more conservative folk felt repelled and threatened—they thought the kids were rioting, and that it was the end of civilization as they knew it. Meanwhile, many young people simply felt misunderstood! Their cult heroes—Elvis, James Dean and Marlon Brando, with their powerful music, fast cars, and motorcycles, echoed their frustration, confusion, and feelings of rebellion, and also provided dangerous, thrilling, role models to admire and emulate. What's more, teenagers now had plenty of money to spend, and this bought them more independence and freedom.

Dream as if you'll live forever,
live as if you'll die today.

James Dean

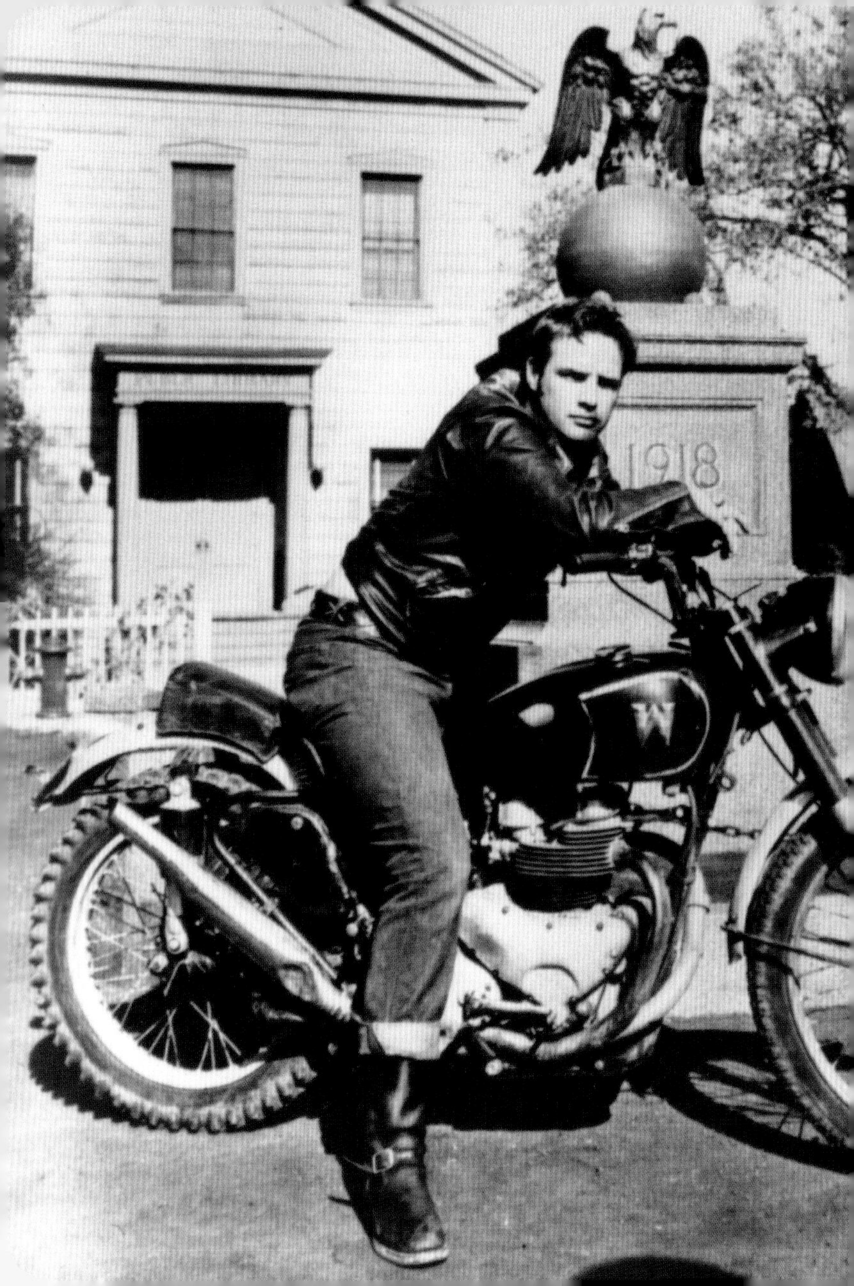
1918

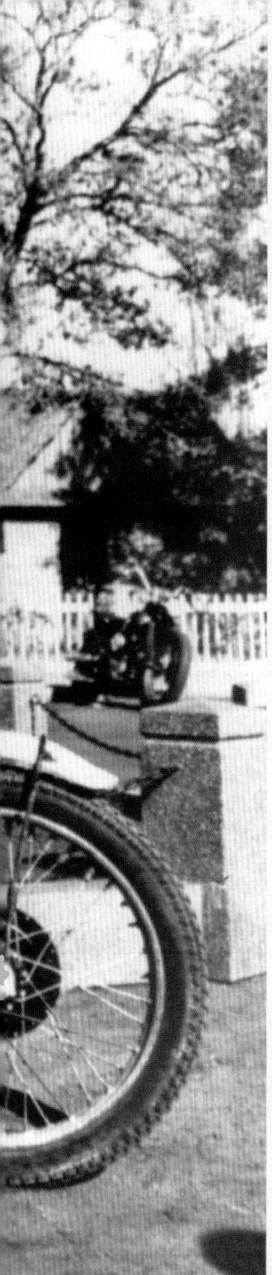

rebels and heroes

They rolled into our lives driving hot rods and Harleys, those movie rebels of the silver screen. And they remained thereafter, in our hearts and memories...The film industry gave birth to an assemblage of 1950s movie rebels; of these icons, James Dean, Marlon Brando and Elvis Presley have proved the most enduring and beloved. In 1954, Brando starred in "The Wild One." It was this film that established him as the irrepressible rebel. As "Johnny," the leader of a motorcycle gang, Brando was the quintessential rebel, decked out in T-shirt, black leather jacket, and motorcycle boots—a uniform that would henceforth symbolize the bad-boy biker's image. Teens began wearing black leather to express feelings of rebellion.

Cookie Curci

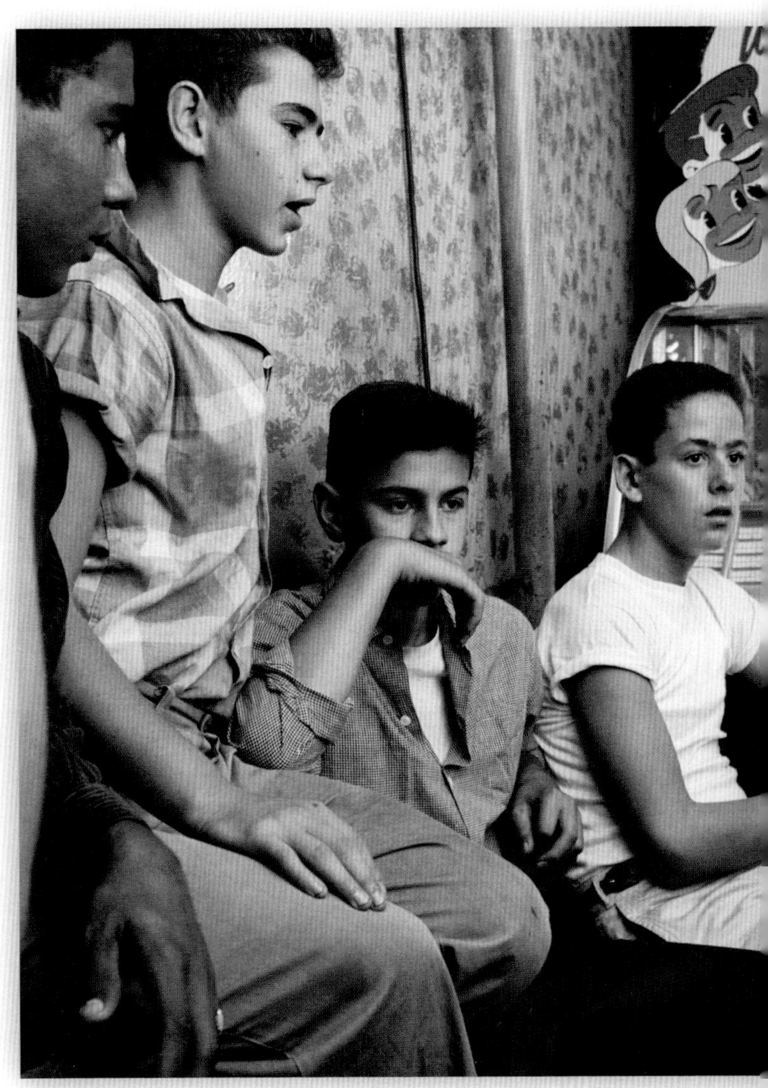

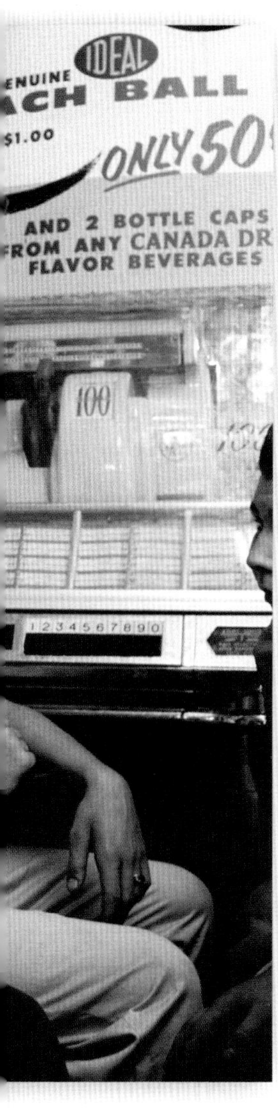

tough guys!

And look at us…we were all dressed like the "Fonz" from "Happy Days" or James Dean in the movie "Rebel Without a Cause"…Yes, it was cheap to dress back then, because every day we wore a white T-shirt with a pair of Levi's, a black wide Buster Brown belt, black engineer boots with steel horseshoe taps....kind of loose to get the right sound as we walk down the halls of good old BHS. The jacket was optional.

Louis J. Barbier

"We just want to look like James Dean!"

the heck with that!

Mayor Hynes (of Hynes Auditorium fame) made a public statement that rock concerts will no longer be tolerated in his city. "They (the promoters) will not be permitted in Boston and no outside promoters need apply (for a license)." Paul Brown (manager of the Boston Arena) added,

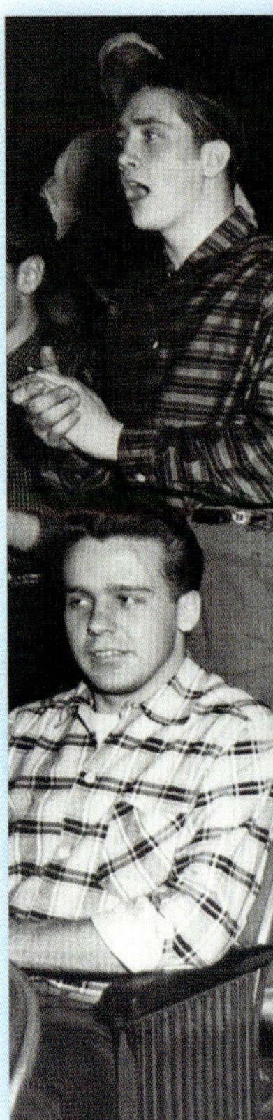

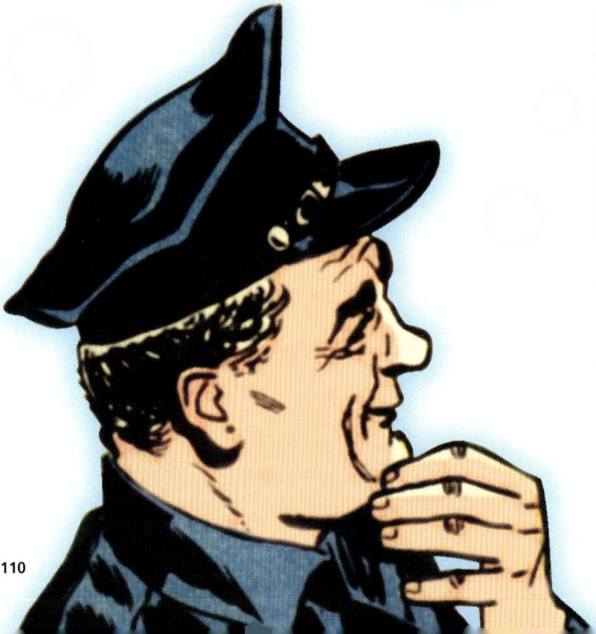

"Kids were standing on chairs and dancing in the aisles the minute the police backs were turned. The building was dark with only the spotlights on. I said 'the heck with that,' and I ordered on the house lights."

Boston Globe, May 6, 1958

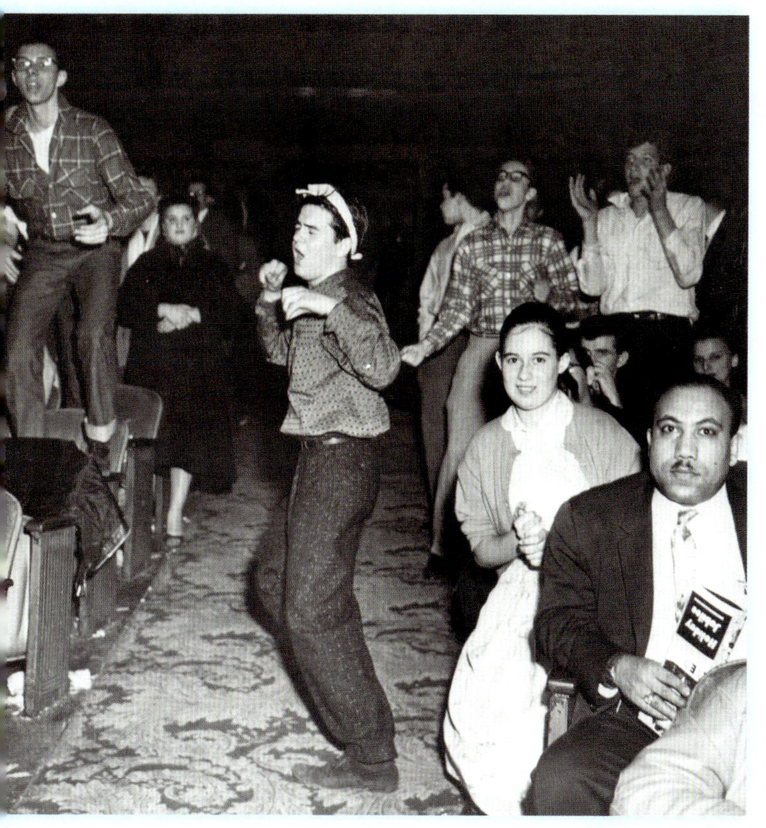

what's allowed?

On the question of how much spending money youngsters should have, parents agreed that one dollar a week was a reasonable limit for boys and girls in grade 9; two dollars a week for grades 10 and 11; and three dollars for grade 12.

Cleveland Plain Dealer, January 2, 1956

"Don't know much about history!"

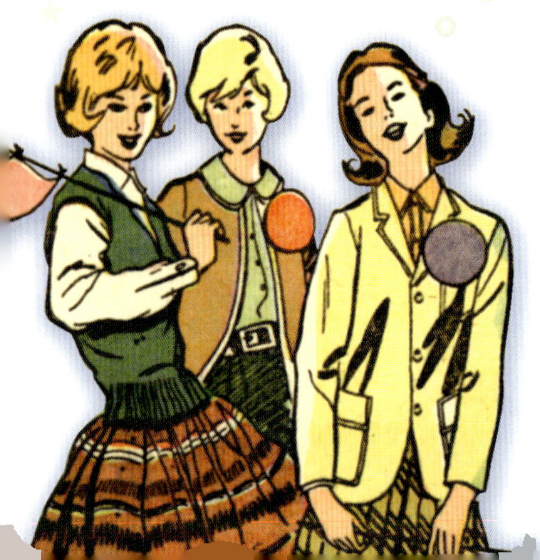

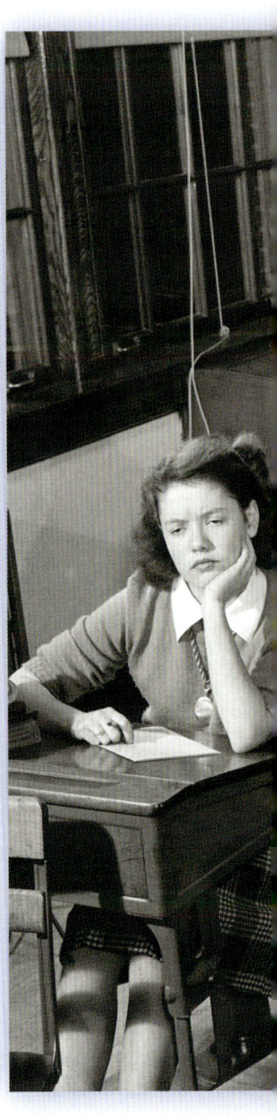

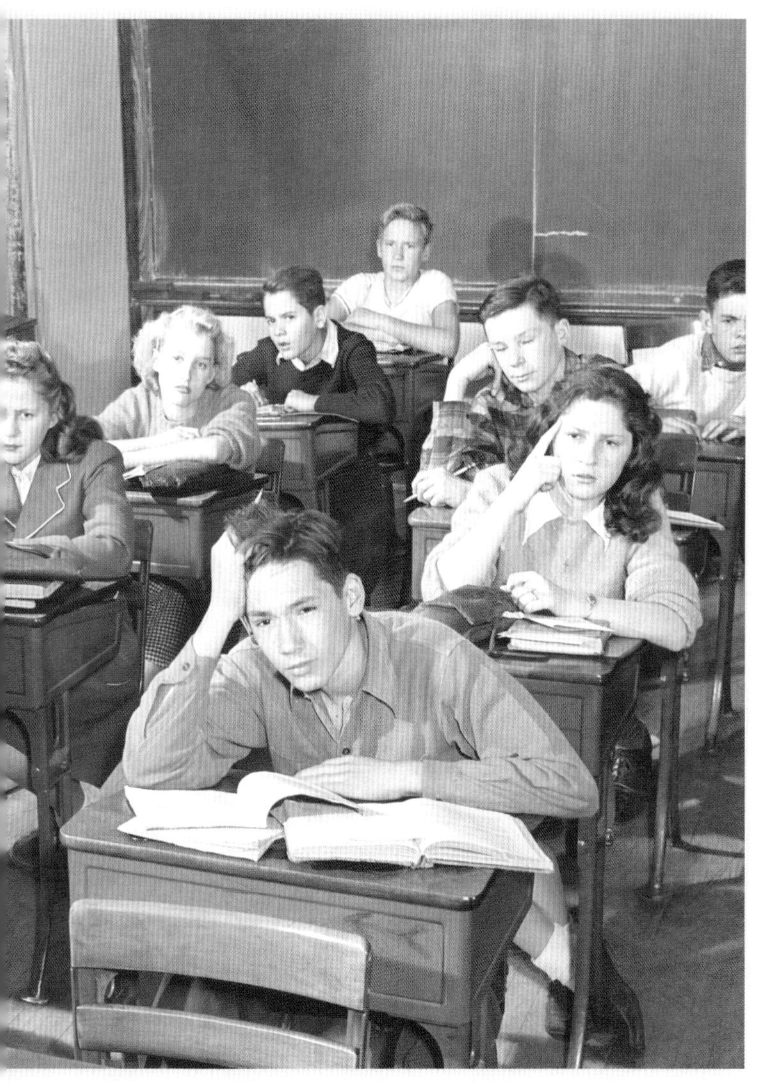

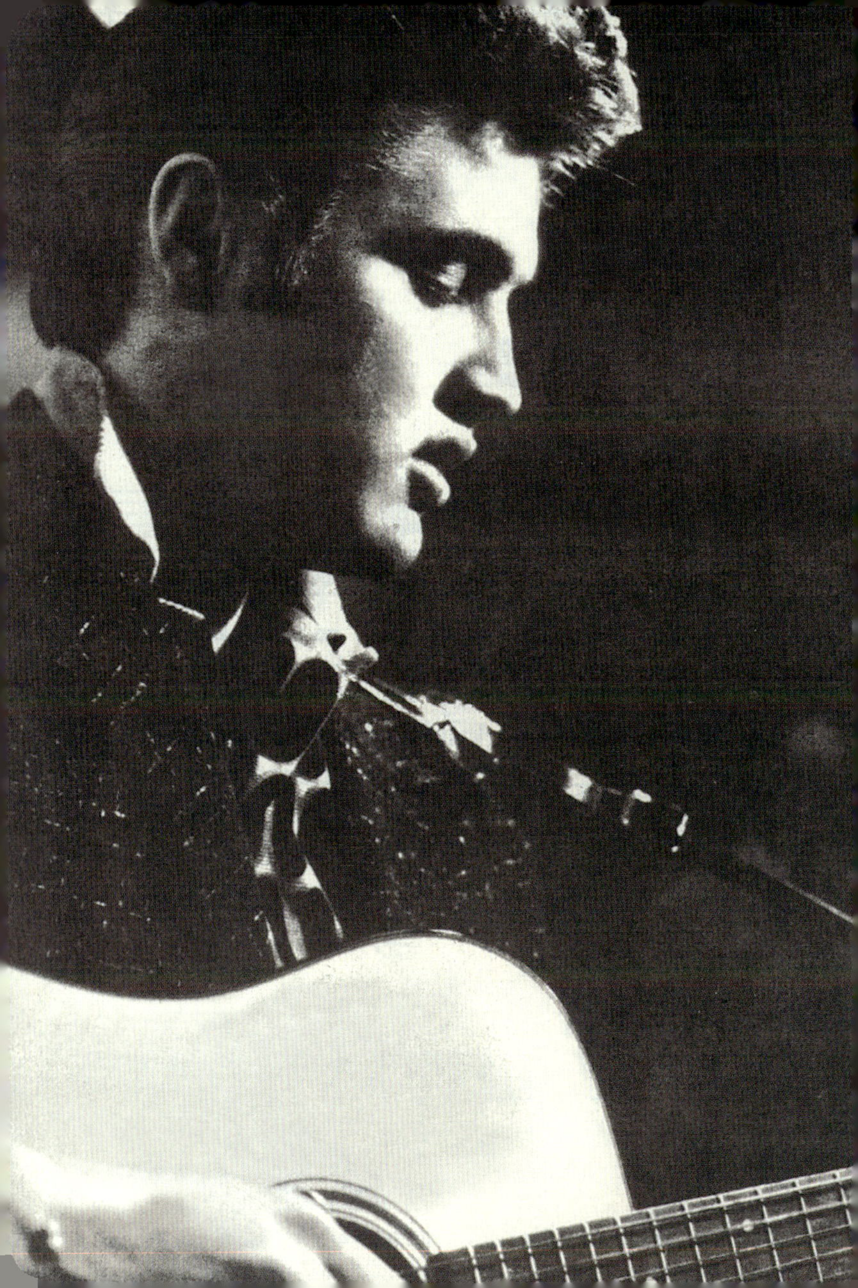

moral corruption

"Stuff like that gets me weary," Presley said, pointing to the headlines. On page one on large bold type was a story headlined "Pastor flays Elvis. Elvis Presley is morally insane." The story, quoting the clergyman, said in part, "The belief of unholy pleasure has sent the morals of the nation down to rock bottom and the crowning addition to this day's corruption is Elvis Presleyism." Next to that story, still on that same page was another: A prominent Los Angeles judge, commenting on a serious case of juvenile delinquency, said, "It is strange that in all these cases involving boys under age, everyone has been wearing an Elvis Presley haircut."...Suddenly Elvis turned to me and said, "If I thought for one minute that I'd contributed to juvenile delinquency I'd go back to driving a truck."

Photoplay, 1957

what it's really like

I try to imitate life. The picture deals with the problems of modern youth. It is the romanticized conception of the juvenile that causes much of our trouble with misguided youth nowadays. I think the one thing this picture shows that's new is the psychological disproportion of the kids' demands on the parents. Parents are often at fault, but the kids have some work to do, too. But you can't show some far off idyllic conception of behavior if you want the kids to come and see the picture. You've got to show what it's really like, and try to reach them on their own grounds.

James Dean

...from an interview at a preview of "Rebel Without a Cause"

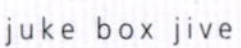

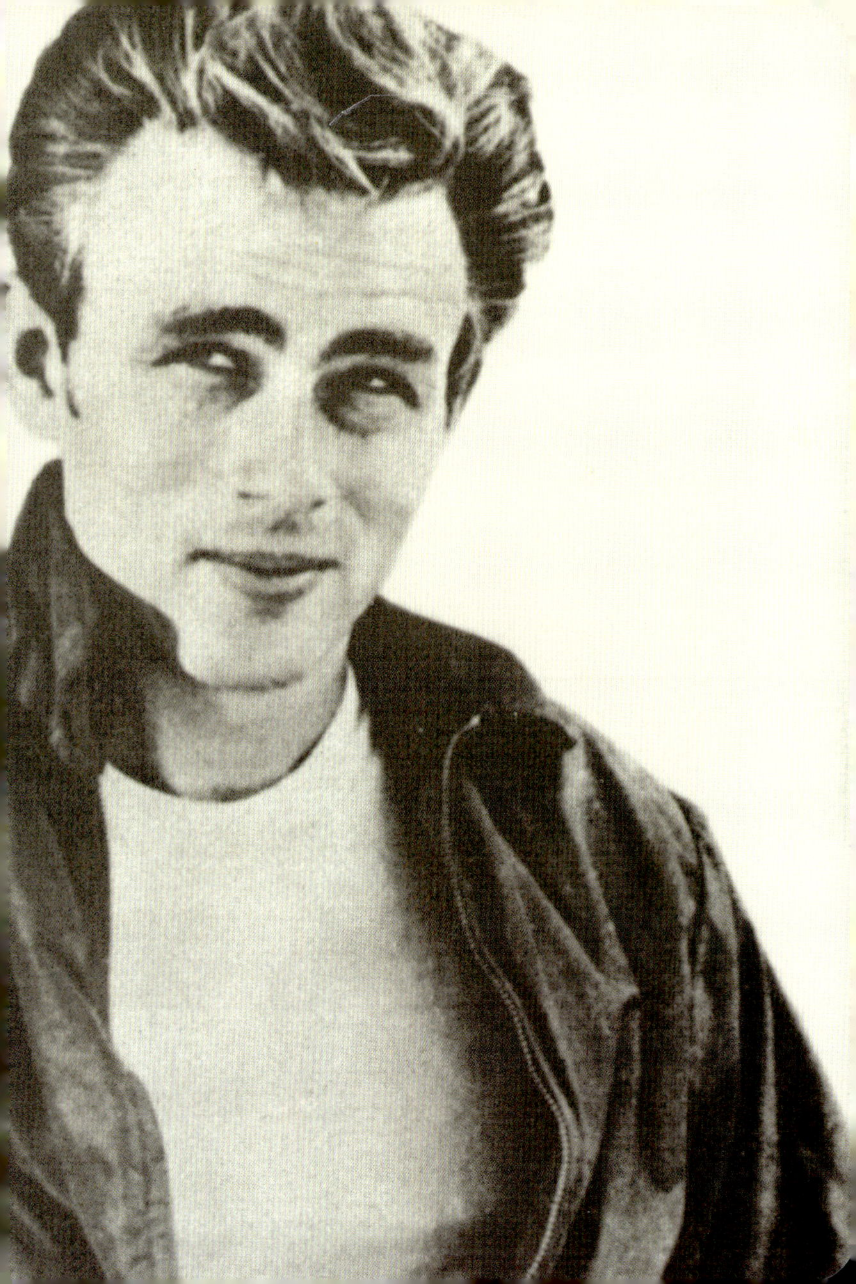

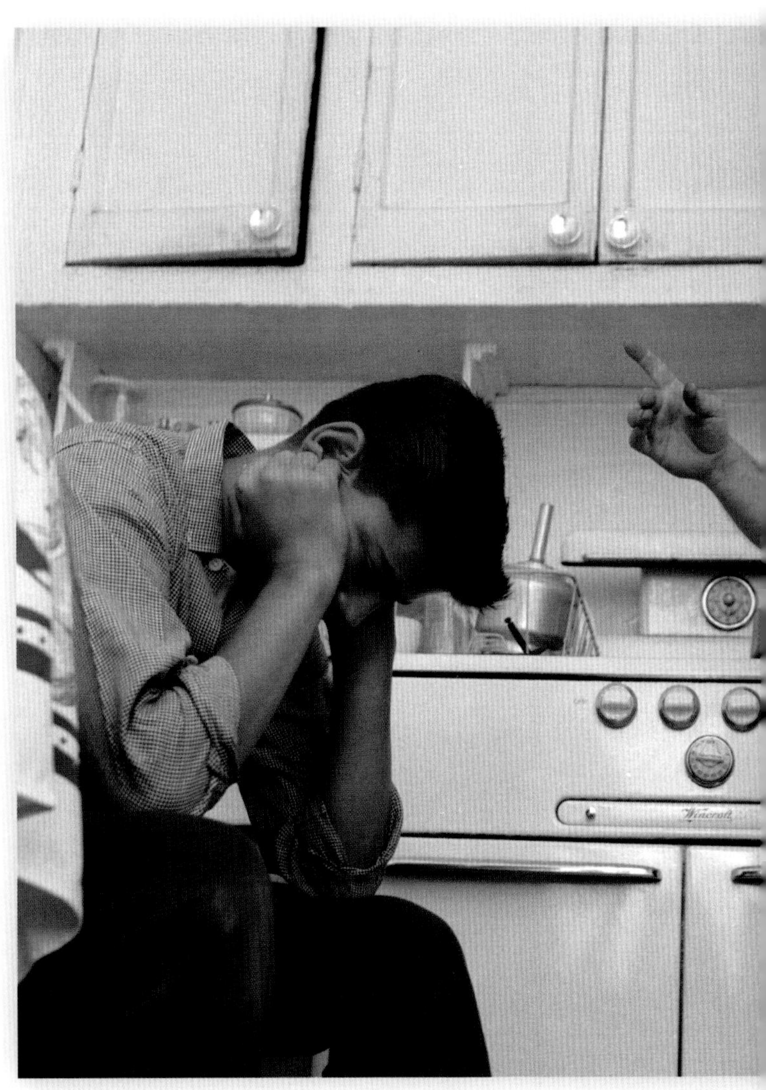

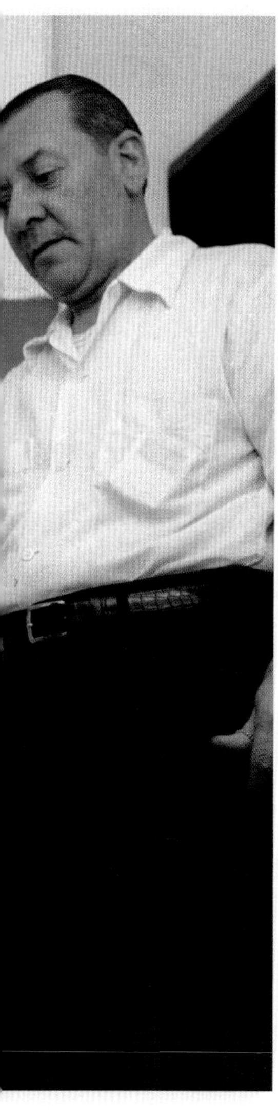

misunderstood?

Ask any teenager who doesn't like being a teenager why, and he'll tell you he's mistreated, misunderstood, unwanted, or unneeded. But we want to disprove his theory. Take, for instance, mistreated. You think you are mistreated, but later you'll find out it was all for your own good and you'll "mistreat" your own teenagers. Misunderstood? Do you really and truly understand yourself? No—if you do you are an exception to the teenage race. Because rarely does a teenager understand himself. So…therefore, how do you expect others to understand you? Unwanted or unneeded? No one is really unwanted or unneeded…if your pet hippopotamus depends on you for his daily food, then aren't you needed? We sorta think that disproves that teenager's theory and helps prove ours—that "It's Great to Be a Teenager!"

J. McC, and M. M.
Pat Boone Magazine, 1959

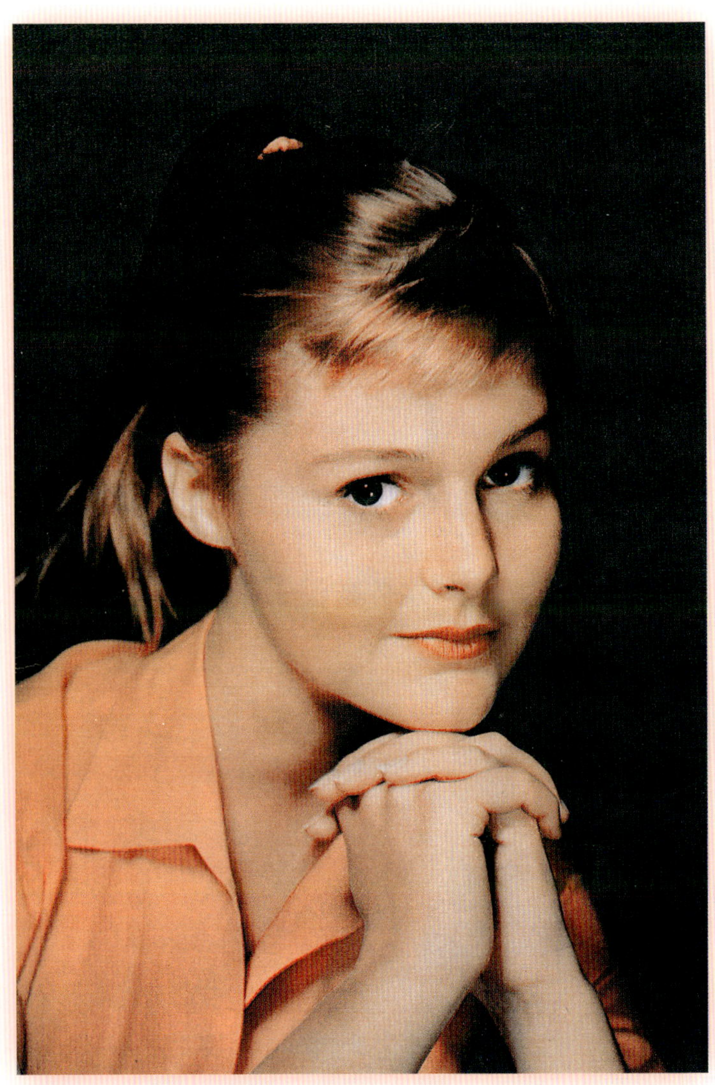

so young, so wise!

Carol Lynley prefers to be called a "young adult" rather than a teenager—and with very good reason. For lovely, blue-eyed Carol is not a teenage divorcee, she doesn't hate her mother, she didn't come from an orphanage, she doesn't feel rejected and unloved, she doesn't have to prove herself by gaining success and recognition, and she isn't an underprivileged juvenile delinquent. Carol herself thinks there is far too much emphasis on youth and its problems today. "All the publicity given to teenage problems is very bad because it makes some teenagers feel forced to grow up," she observes wisely. "You can't be 21 until you are 21, and up till then you are naturally learning, finding out about things, and your character is forming."

Carol Lynley

New Screen News, 1959

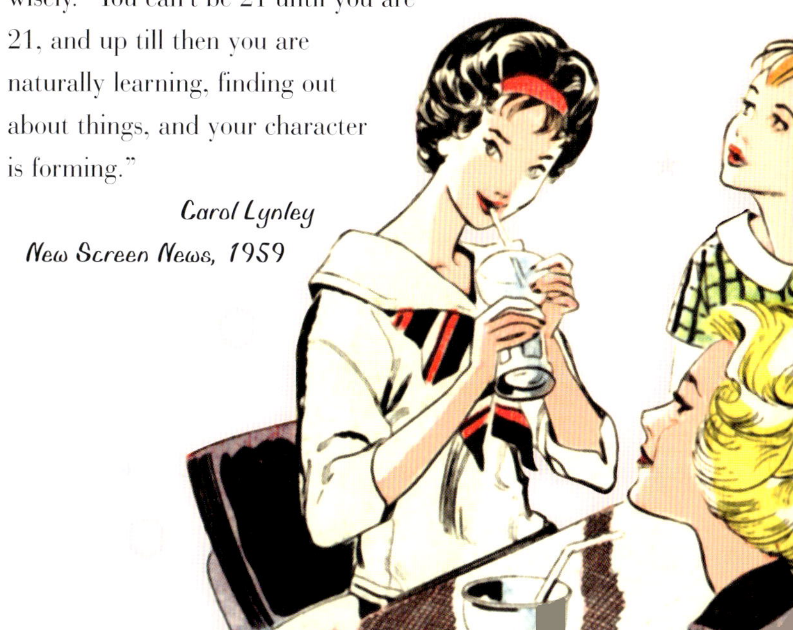

a consuming passion!

It's no news to anybody with teenage relatives that adolescent love for Mr. Alexander Graham Bell's brainchild has been growing in recent years until, in some cases, it has become a consuming passion. Telephoning is actually rivaling televiewing as a recreation in some sets; and, what's more, so great is the adaptive power of the young that a few hardy pioneers are already developing the skills necessary to view a show and simultaneously discuss it by phone with a friend two blocks away.

Dorothy Barclay, New York Times, 1956

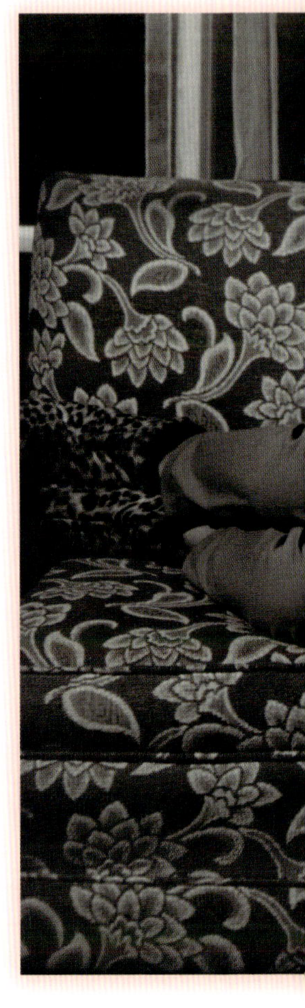

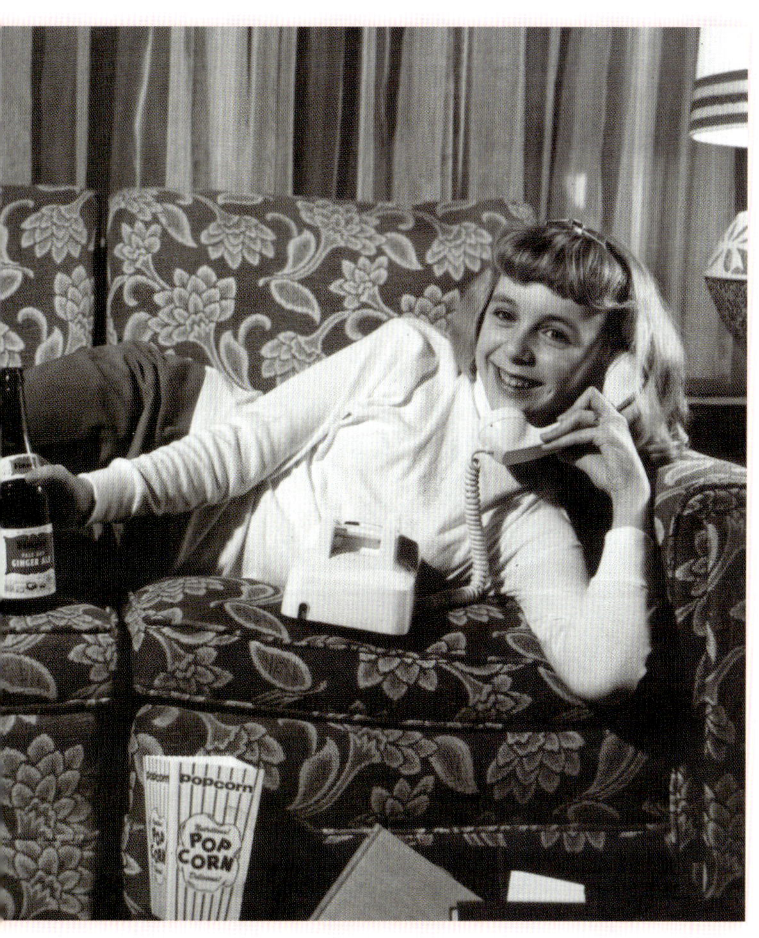
GINGER ALE
popcorn
popcorn
POP CORN
POP CORN

index

Picture credits

GETTY IMAGES: 15; 18; 33; 37; 42; 52; 62; 67; 68;88; 99; 106; 108; 118; 123
CORBIS: 8 also on p. 38; 10; 20; 25; 26; 44; 45; 48; 58; 65; 74; 85; 86; 90; 100; 102; 111; 113
ADVERTISING ARCHIVES: 8, 78 (with permission of The Coca-Cola Company); 104
THE KOBAL COLLECTION: 13 Lucas Film/Coppola Co/Universal/The Kobal Collection
17 Walt Disney Pictures (from "The Horsemasters").
96 Warner Brothers Pictures (from "The Dark at the Top of the Stairs")
Jukebox pictures on front cover and pages 2, 28 and 29 supplied courtesy of the Wurlitzer Jukebox Company

Acknowledgments

9 *Starlife* Magazine, 1959; 11 Samantha S; 12 Larry Martin; 14 Mike Forrester; 16 Lisa Johnson; 21 Carl Gustafson; 22/23, 76/77, 92, 94/95 Miranda Smith; 24, 59 and 98 Reba and J.B Criner; 28 Jo Stafford/*Billboard*, 1958; 31 Rita Murphy; 32 Tom Lowell; 34 Meg Sutton; 36 Jaynie Allen; 37 *Pat Boone Magazine*, 1960; 39 Cindy Morrison; 41 Louise R. Franks; 44/45 Rod Owen; 46 *Time* Magazine, May 15, 1956; 49 *Movie Stars Parade*, 1958; 51 Carl Perkins; 53 Tony Papard; 54 *Movie TV Secrets*, April 1959; 57 Excerpt from *Boy meets Girl* 1959; 61 Brandon de Wilde, *Photoplay*, 1959; 63 Jeff Klinkenburg, *St. Petersburg Times*; 65 Jeff Dillon; 66 Jess Parker; 69 Ted Morrison; 70 Carol Lynley, *Pat Boone Magazine*, 1960; 73 *Photoplay*, 1959; 75 Excerpt from Margaret Mitchell's *Gone with the Wind*; 79 Bobby Vee; 81 Patti Smith; 82 Bruce Walker; 85 Jon Rutherford; 87 Mel Brodecky; 89 Annie L. George; 91 Mary Lou Shepherd; 97 Ginger Farrell; 103 Sue Trimmer; 104 James Dean; 107 Cookie Curci; 109 Louis J. Barbier; 111 *Boston Globe*, May 6, 1958; 113 *Cleveland Plain Dealer*, January 2, 1956; 115 *Photoplay*, 1957; 116 James Dean; 119 J. McC, and M.M. *Pat Boone Magazine*, 1959; 121 Carol Lynley, *New Screen News*, 1959; Dorothy Barclay, *New York Times*, 1956